EMPOWERED BY THE UNIFORM

Ismon Marroquin

◆ FriesenPress

One Printers Way
Altona, MB R0G 0B0
Canada

www.friesenpress.com

Copyright © 2023 by Ismon Marroquin
First Edition — 2023

All rights reserved.

No part of this publication may be reproduced in any form, or by any means, electronic or mechanical, including photocopying, recording, or any information browsing, storage, or retrieval system, without permission in writing from FriesenPress.

ISBN
978-1-03-916652-3 (Hardcover)
978-1-03-916651-6 (Paperback)
978-1-03-916653-0 (eBook)

1. POLITICAL SCIENCE, CORRUPTION & MISCONDUCT

Distributed to the trade by The Ingram Book Company

HUNTING SEASON	**67**
Always Eager to Pull the Trigger	67
After Killing a Man Police Refuse a Breathalyzer	70
Man Killed by Police in Front of Many Witnesses.	73
RCMP Officers Killed an Innocent Newcomer at Vancouver Airport	74
Man Trapped Like a Rabbit	78
A call for Help Turns Deadly for an Innocent Man	80
Police Killed a Teenager and After Tasered his Cadaver	82
A Man Attacked by RCMP Officers Dies of a Brain Hemorrhage	84
Young Man Killed by RCMP with a Rain of Bullets	87
Community Concerned for Family of Man Shot by RCMP Officers	89
A Man is Killed by Police in Front of His Girlfriend	91
Police Killed a Man Who Needed Help	93
Police Kill Man with Depression Instead of Assisting Him	94
Police Kill a Hurt Teenage Girl Needing Assistance	95
SWAT Team Kills a Black Man with an M16 Rifle	97
Police Officers Kill a Man Who Held a Toy Gun in His Hand.	98
Woman Calls Police to Help her Husband, but They Give Her His Cadaver	100
Thompson Police Leave a Man Dead and a Woman Injured	102
Man Chased, Arrested, and Handcuffed by Police, Later Died in Custody	104
Lack of English Could Result in Death	105
Taxi Driver Killed by Police After Brutal Torture	107
Indigenous Young Man Killed by Police	108
Police Pepper Spray a Man and Killed Him While he is Temporarily Blind	109
Indigenous Man Walking Suspiciously is Killed by Police	110
A Killing in Good Faith	112

Police Chased a Man with Weapons Drawn and Killed Him   113
Three Indigenous Men Died in Custody   115

CROOKS ENFORCING THE LAW   **119**

Two Tiers of Citizens   119
A web of Corruption Involving Some of Our Finest   121
Is Canada's Police Forces Getting Dirtier?   123
Police Disagree with Sentence   124
Police Officer Guilty of Brutal Assault   125
Woman Handcuffed to a Table in the Police Station   126
Nobody is Safe When Police Are Around   127
Mr. Brown Cannot Drive a Fancy Car   128
Brutal Beating for a Case of Beer   129
City Police Assaulted a Man Close to Concert Hall   130
Chief of First Nations Community Assaulted by RCMP Officers   131
Teenager Holding a Machete Was Shot by Police   133
Opportunity for Assault Taken by Off Duty Police Officer   135
Welcome to the Capital of the Friendly Province   136
Police Attack a South African Man   137
Off Duty Officers Accused of Ramming
a Car and Assaulting the Driver   138
Acquitted Man Sues the Police Over Brutal Assault   140
Police Pepper Spray an Epileptic Man Inside an Ambulance   141
Working Mother Killed by Drunk Off Duty Police Officer   142
Video Tells the Truth about a Police Officer Beating   143
Police Should Get Criminals, Not Create Them   144
City Police Fail to Notify Watchdog About Injuries   145
Four Police Officers Assaulted a Family in a Hotel Room   147

EPILOGUE   **149**

REFERENCES   **155**

PREFACE

When I arrived in Canada accompanied by my wife and three children, I was excited for the opportunities I expected for myself and my family, despite not knowing any English, I came to give my family the best that I could, so that they would be happy and prepared for their future. We were ready to face the challenges our new life would present to us. However, we realized that life would be difficult for everybody due to the language, climate, and our lack of knowledge of Canadian systems. We met a guy from our own country, who had arrived about three years before us. He told us that he regularly visited many Spanish-speaking families, so his friends called him "Chucho" (dog). He did not help us in any way, but he often showed up at our home at dinner time without an invitation. He scheduled his time in such a way that he did this with all the families he visited each week, and he never missed a weekend or special occasion that included free drinks and food – all without an invitation, of course.

About a month after we had moved to the city, and seen many interesting places, including City Hall, where some police officers were walking around, we were chatting with Chucho about the system. I told him that I was very impressed with the nice behaviour of police officers, who seemed to be well educated and respectful with the public. Chucho laughed hard and told me that I had gotten a false impression about them, because police officers in this country are as bad as in our own. Then he added, "wait a little longer to see for yourself". He was right. I did not have to wait too long for an ugly experience with those guys.

One day my wife and I were walking on the sidewalk along a busy downtown street when suddenly, I was pulled from behind by two police officers, who immediately tried to take me into their cruiser without any explanation. As a natural reaction, I resisted their effort to force me into their vehicle because I had not done anything wrong; besides, I was a newcomer who did not understand the language, so I did not know what they were saying. Within a matter of seconds, I had flashbacks about the way in which the citizens of my country were regularly kidnapped and never seen again.

Fortunately, and by mere coincidence, Chucho was walking on the other sidewalk and witnessed what was going on. He came over and asked the police officer to explain to him what the problem was, since we were newcomers who didn't understand any English. The police officer told him that the night before, somebody who looked like me had committed a crime in Nova Scotia, and they were helping with the case. They asked for my passport, and when I gave it to them, one of them went to a nearby business to make a phone call, after which they let me go.

After that incident my wife and I went to the Safety Building, which was the police headquarters at the time. I intended to file a complaint about the behaviour of those officers, as at that point I still believed that the police were professionals and well educated. However, that experience was just as bad as the incident itself, as the person at the front desk was arrogant, rude, and completely lacking in people skills. He ignored us from the moment we walked in; I felt upset and embarrassed, even though, by then we were already aware that discrimination was normal with most city officers, as we had been told by others who had immigrated before us. My personal experience that day changed my original opinion about the police in general. Since then, I have become increasingly convinced that racism and discrimination are normal in this country, despite the authorities trying to deny it. Friends told us many stories about the police stopping people in the middle of the street to check them, and sometimes making arrests for no apparent reason, especially if they were dealing with Indigenous people or immigrants of all races. I also heard that the police department was the most racist and discriminatory of all government agencies in the country.

It was a sad day for me because my confidence in the system was broken and almost destroyed. But, it was a good experience for the future, teaching me to be vigilant and more careful with my whole family. I felt humiliated, because, before this incident, I had never had any encounters with the police, but from then on, I was more interested in reading the newspapers; and paying close attention to the behaviour of those City employees in charge of enforcing the law, I started saving newspaper articles related to police officers. Over the years as I was able to read and understand more English, I learned a lot of things concerning the police; and the other institutions working with them. There were so many problems that I decided to keep a record of the more severe incidents involving the police in the country, as I thought that maybe some day, I could write a book about my own and others' experiences with law enforcement. Within a short time, I had collected several news articles about the many abuses committed by these public servants, but I never got the courage to write the book – until now, thanks to an encounter with a police officer.

I guess I have been lucky because in all my years living in this country, I have only been pulled over three times by the police. Two of hose times happened more than thirty years ago, and the other was the one that gave me the courage I needed to start writing this book.

I have always been a careful driver, and I always make sure that I have my driver's licence on me, and the vehicle registration documents inside the glove box. However, on February 11, 2021, I took my pick up truck to the dealership to replace the passenger side airbag inflator. Before taking the truck to the shop, I removed everything from the glove box. When I got the vehicle back, I forgot to put everything back in the compartment again. I parked the vehicle in front of my house and did not move it for one whole week, as the temperature outside was between -40 and -45°C. On February 18, when the temperature improved, I took the truck for an errand and had the misfortune of being pulled over by constable M., who gave me a ticket for $113.00 for not having the registration documents with me. Although Mr. M was polite and respectful, without knowing it, he reminded me that I had a book to write about the police. With this book, I want to tell my story and those of countless Canadians about countless interactions with the police. I hope that one day they will improve their culture.

Other than my personal experiences, everything contained in this book is part of the public record. My intention is to help in some way to restore the credibility of police officers in the eyes of society. The credibility of law enforcement has been seriously damaged due to the actions of some police officers who do not care about the reputation of their institution. There has been wide media coverage in recent years of police actions involving discrimination, racism, and aggression. These officers do not appear to understand that their bad actions affect the whole institution, in which, without a doubt, many police officers are doing their job with respect, integrity, and consideration of the well being of the citizens they serve every day.

I decided to title this book *Empowered by the Uniform* because many people seem to change their personality when they are wearing a uniform, as the uniform allows them to become who they really are. When we see people in police uniforms, we immediately know what we can expect from them; unfortunately, their behaviour often gives us a sense of fear, insecurity, and lack of confidence. While they might feel proud wearing that uniform, the public's trust depends on the way these officers perform their duties. Without the uniform, they are normal people and can mix with civilians without anybody recognizing them. I think some members of the police force go through a personality transformation when they put that uniform on; they become different when in a position of authority and carrying a gun, or any kind of weapon. It almost seems like they feel they are above the law.

Over the several years that I have spent following crimes involving police officers who were on duty or off duty when the crimes were committed, they have rarely, if ever been found guilty of their trespasses. In other words, it seems like they enjoy immunity and impunity. They always seem to have the support of their supervisors, lawyers, institutions related to their job, and sometimes the courts. That conflictive situation will be explained in this book using real examples, hoping that police officers who have vocation for the job, keep or improve their good behaviour as an example to their coworkers who may not have vocation to hold that delicate position. These officers without vocation are an easy instrument to denigrate the whole institution with their deplorable behavior whenever they are dealing with people who are members of visible minorities. Police officers should be admired, respected, and appreciated for conviction and never for fear, intimidation, or aggressions. All police officers must understand that they are part of the society, giving clear examples of obeying the law they are upholding. They should never ever think that they are above the law and have the right of humiliating civilians, destroying, or taking away their rights without legal consequences.

The Author

PERSONAL EXPERIENCES

Our First Taste of Discrimination

Years ago, when my children were teenagers and we were newcomers in this country, one of them insisted on getting a new bicycle. All his friends had bicycles, and he wanted to ride with them. Although we did not have much money, we made the effort to get him a bike. Unfortunately, a few weeks later somebody cut the chain securing the bike to a pole and stole the bike, leaving my son sad and frustrated. We saved up more money and were able to buy him a second bike, but this time we also bought a heavier chain so that it would not run the same fate as the first bike. As luck would have it, this one also got stolen in the same way as the first one – the thieves cut the chain and took the bike. My son and I were devastated and upset, given that within a month, two brand new bicycles had been stolen from him. Fortunately, I had kept the serial numbers for both bicycles.

One day, a friend told me that the police had a place on Logan Avenue, where they kept every bicycle they recovered, so, with the serial number on hand, I went to that storage facility to see if we could get information about the bikes. I asked my son to go with me in case the police wanted to ask him questions about the bicycles. When we arrived, we found a large garage with lots of bicycles hanging from the ceiling. We said hello to the police officer at the desk, but he did not answer. Because he was wearing a police officer uniform and had a badge, a baton, front identification, and a monogram, we thought he was the right person to ask for information. When we approached the desk, I proceeded to tell him that we were looking for a couple of bicycles that had been stolen from my son a few weeks earlier and that we had the serial number of each bicycle.

1

Ismon Marroquin

The officer did not even have the courtesy to look at us, much less say anything. He motioned with his lips in the direction of the bicycles and said two words that, unfortunately, we did not understand, as we were still new to the country. It was evident that he did not appreciate my strong accent and the way I was speaking, which made me think that he was racist and discriminating against us. I felt upset, humiliated, and offended because somebody who could be the face of the city, did not have the courtesy to treat us with dignity and respect. Over thirty-five years ago, that insolent, arrogant, and uneducated police officer marked my soul for ever, because I can not forget his regrettable attitude on behalf of the police institution, it made me think that all of them were prepared in the same way. My impression was terrible because, as a professional with a university degree, having been a university professor, I had to tolerate the insolence of a Mr. nobody only because he had the advantage of the language and was wearing a uniform that was staining the city he was representing. With his behaviour he was intimidating and scaring people with a language disadvantage. He treated us exactly the way I had been treated years earlier when I had visited the Public Safety Building after being grabbed from behind by the police officer who thought I looked like the person who had committed a crime in another part of the country earlier that week.

This was one of many situations in which the police did not show any basic decency when dealing with the public. He had treated us like animals, his inability to deal with people in a respectful way prevented him from seeing that we were there looking for help from a public servant. We were human beings like himself and deserved the same respect he expected from us. We left empty-handed, without even the hope that there was a way to find those bikes.

Little by little I was learning about the way police officers work in the city and how they treat visible minorities. Even with my lack of English, my university education had given me a complete picture of the police department with each situation I encountered. And while not every police officer is rude and arrogant, the few that fall in those categories affect the reputation of the entire institution. Maybe they think that every person who comes from another country is stupid, based on the way they speak English. But among those people being discriminated against by the police are doctors, lawyers, journalists, engineers, teachers, scientists, social workers, and more. These newcomers understand what is going on, even if they can not speak the language.

Emergency Calls Never Attended

My family was living in North Kildonan and renting a duplex house. Our neighbour was a very nice woman in her seventies, whose son lived with her. One winter night around mid-night we were already sleeping and suddenly heard a loud noise at the neighbour's house. We realized that there was a fight going on – somebody was hitting the walls, screaming, yelling, and crying. Thinking this was a serious situation and that somebody could get seriously hurt, I called 911. When I explained what was going on the attendant told me that the police would arrive in a few minutes, but they never did. The fight continued to escalate, so about half an hour later I called again and told them that the police had not showed up. Once again, the attendant told me that the police would arrive in a few minutes, but they never did. Then I looked out the window and saw the elderly neighbour walking outside without a jacket, so I ran out with a jacket and gave it to her. She told me that her grandson was beating her son because they were both drinking. When she got back inside her house, I called 911 again. They told me that the police would arrive in a few minutes, but again, they never did. We waited for about three hours, and they never showed up; not later, not the next day, not ever.

In retrospect, I am glad they never showed up, because my neighbours were indigenous, and, based on what I have seen over the years, somebody might have been killed that night. Throughout this book, I document many cases in which the police were called to an emergency but, instead of trying to de-escalate the situation, they used their guns, tasers, or other aggressive means to handle the problem. Often, they only aggravated the situation; in some cases, people were killed by officers using these weapons. It seems that some of them are quick to use their pistol, taser, or other weapon, and while I can not say if that approach is part of their training, I think it shows that they are ill-prepared to handle the needs of the community. This leads me to think that the relationship between police departments and the public, particularly indigenous people, or minority groups, will never improve. There are too many situations in which a police officer has killed someone they were supposed to protect when called to a crisis in a home. And instead of being punished, the officers have been placed on paid leave while an internal investigation is conducted. Most of the time, the investigation finds no wrongdoing by the officers.

Throughout the years, I have learned that many people are afraid of the police and prefer to stay far away of them; their uniform is scary and does not inspire trust, particularly for some groups of the population.

Winning a Case in Court but Losing Anyway

When I first started my business, a customer came in to get her car fixed. She wanted to pay by cheque, but I told her that I preferred other forms of payment. After a small discussion during which she assured me that her cheques were good, I decided to accept her cheque. However, she asked for a favor – to split the payment between two payments so she gave me two cheques – one was to be deposited immediately and the other one the following week.

I went to the bank to deposit the first cheque and kept the other one for later, as she had instructed. As I was getting ready to go to the bank the following week to deposit the second cheque, the mail arrived. One of the envelopes was from the bank, and sure enough, her first cheque was inside – it had bounced. Not only had I lost the payment, but now I also had to pay bank charges for the bounced cheque. I called the customer, and she told me that there must be a mistake and apologized. She promised that she would be at the shop promptly to fix the problem, but she never showed up and never answered my telephone calls again.

After several failed attempts to recover the money, I decided to go to the police to file a complaint or claim against her. Once again, I encountered the typical discrimination that by then I had become familiar with. As I approached the officer at the front desk, he did not even make an effort to look at me. As I explained the reason for my visit, he kept going about his business, reading some papers on the desk. Then I showed him both cheques I had received from the customer, and as he briefly glanced at them, he proceeded to say that the police did not care about those kinds of problems. He did not bother to take any notes about my report. He just told me to go to small claims court. I did not ask any other questions, for fear of getting in trouble with him. It was obvious that he was not interested in helping me, much less investigating the case.

I lamented having wasted my time going there, but it was so much money, I needed to do something. I started going between institutions, trying to figure out how to recover the money. As I was a sole proprietor and had no help at the time, I had to close my business while I was trying to get the problem sorted out. I soon discovered that the loss would be more than just the money that the customer had basically stolen from me. I now had to pay for every application I filled out trying to get my money. And as if that was not enough, I also had to serve the customer with court documents myself. And all this time, I would have to close the business while I was doing this running around.

I was surprised by all these requirements because in developing countries this type of work is usually done by the police. They can enforce any order from the courts, and they make sure that the accuser and the accused are present in court on the day of their hearing. I wasted a lot of time trying to find this customer, but I was finally able to serve her with the court document.

When the court date arrived, I showed up early to make sure I did not get any surprises; she never showed up, so, another hearing was set for another day. The next time, she failed to show up again, so the judge ruled in my favour. I was very happy about this, as I thought I would have my money soon, but I was wrong. This was just another step in my long fight to get justice. The judge asked me to talk to the Sheriff, who would tell me what to do next. The sheriff told me that I needed to find out what kind of assets or properties she had so that I could recover my money that way. I told him about the car I had fixed, so he said he would send somebody to get the car as soon as possible. Unfortunately, that never happened, and every time I reached out to him to inquire about my case, he would give me all kinds of excuses and explanations.

Ismon Marroquin

One day, I received a letter in the mail informing me, that this customer had applied for bankruptcy. In the same envelope was a letter informing me of how many other creditors were in my situation.

I knew I could have recovered my money had the sheriff impounded the vehicle when I first spoke to him. I was so upset I decided to write a letter to the Minister of Justice to explain everything that had happened and to complain about the sheriff. Soon after I sent the letter, I received a call from the sheriff, who apologized for not getting the vehicle. He explained that he had not impounded the vehicle because he did not think the car would cover the amount the woman owed me. I told him it was up to me to decide that, and even if the price of the car had not covered the entire debt, anything would have been better than nothing.

It was a very bad experience for me, and I was frustrated because I felt the judicial system had failed me. If I had known in advance how the system works, I would have cut my losses from the moment the customer had stolen that money. The justice system failed me in such a way that it seemed like it had been designed with the purpose of failing people; every step was perfectly deficient, from the police officer's attitude to the sheriff's careless behaviour. My whole experience with the justice system was a waste of time and money.

Another Proof of Discrimination by Police

When I first opened my small business, I had customers from different countries. Many of them were newcomers looking for an affordable and safe place to live. When it came to fixing their vehicles, some of them preferred installing recycled parts on their cars, and when they needed special equipment, they came to my shop. I was always happy to help them. One day a customer came in, who wanted us to install a recycled part in his car; he asked me to charge for the labour and do the job for him, as my shop had the required equipment. I told him that we did not install used parts because sometimes they were defective, and the customer would blame me for the condition of the part. He said if the part was not good, we would not be responsible, and he would deal with the supplier, I did the work and he left.

The next day he showed up complaining that the part was not working properly; I reminded him of what I had told him the day before, but to make him happy, I did the work again for free and recommended that he get another part. He agreed and left. Incredibly, the next day he appeared complaining again. I told him that if he did not get another part, his problem would go on and on, and there was nothing else I could do. He started yelling at me like crazy person, asking for free work one more time. He parked his car in front of the shop blocking the entrance and refused to move it to let other customers enter and exit the shop. To avoid more problems with him, I put the car on the hoist and showed him that my work had been done well, so, if he insisted on having that part in his car, the problem would remain. I also told him that it was the last time I would be doing free work on his car.

He promised not to come back, however, he showed up the next day, yelling and demanding attention. When I refused to work for free on his car, he said that he would kill me, and then he picked up a plastic chair and smashed it on the floor. I called the police but did not get an answer. When he realized I was calling, he left screaming and repeating that he would kill me. I regretted ever letting that guy into my shop, but when I had first seen him, he had not given me any indication of being aggressive. I decided to report the threats to the police. I went to the nearest police station where I found an officer at the front desk reading a newspaper. I said, "good afternoon, sir", but he did not answer my greeting. I was already familiar with this behaviour. I stood in front of him, waiting for him to ask me what I needed, but that did not happen.

After about seven minutes of standing in front of him, I decided to leave the station convinced that it was useless to wait any longer. I went back to my shop, upset and thinking about the systemic discrimination suffered by visible minorities, especially Indigenous people who have faced discrimination since the white people arrived on this land. I was sorrowful because I was yet to receive courteous treatment from these uniformed public servants.

Ismon Marroquin

Discrimination is a Fact

During the time that I was running my business, I learned that in any kind of business, the owner must keep a sharp eye because there are always thieves trying to steal something in different ways, even if they appear to be good people.

One day a guy came to my shop and asked for some work to be done on his car; while my employees were doing the work, the customer talked to me in a very charming way. I never thought that he could be a dangerous person. My policy was that after finishing the work, the mechanics would go for a test drive to make sure there were no problems with the work done. After that, they would put the keys in a designated place to give me the chance to bill the customer and give the keys to him/her myself. That day while I was preparing the bill for the customer, the mechanic came back to the shop following the test drive. Thinking that the man had already paid, as he had been in the waiting area most of the time, he gave the keys to him. Immediately after receiving the keys, he ran away as fast as he could.

When I asked the mechanic to tell the customer that his bill was ready, he told me that he was already gone. Because everything happened in a matter of seconds, I called 911. When I informed the operator what had happened, she told me that for that kind of problem, I had to call the police directly. I called the police right away, and the officer asked me some questions. Then he said, "hold on", I waited, because I assumed he was taking some kind of action and would inform me as soon as he had information about the thief, but that was not the case. Time was running while I waited, and I could not do anything else because the police officer had left me stuck with the telephone in my hand. After five minutes I started getting worried. Another five minutes passed by, and the officer still did not come back to the phone. I did not hang up because I expected to receive some information any minute. After fifteen minutes, I was convinced that the police officer had left me waiting on purpose. I could hear noises from the other end the whole time I was waiting; sometimes voices and people laughing. After twenty minutes I understood that it was useless to keep waiting. I knew that the officer had decided to ignore me, a situation I was already accustomed to when dealing with the police. The police officer who received my telephone call decided to ignore me, maybe because he did not like my strong accent, without even considering that I was paying and collecting taxes to pay the high salaries of public servants like him. After waiting twenty minutes with the telephone at my ear, realizing that I was a victim of abuse and discrimination, I decided to keep waiting until somebody decided to check what was going on with the telephone or hang it up.

For some people this might be hard to believe, but I decided to hang up after waiting seventy minutes for the police officer who supposedly was handling my call. I am sure that many people in the Indigenous communities and other minorities have experienced similar treatment by police officers due to their personal appearance or their accent. No doubt that in my case, the police officer who left me waiting seventy minutes did not like my strong accent and did not care to show me his irresponsible attitude. Those kinds of servants are destroying the credibility of the police forces and damaging its relationship with society.

I am sure that somewhere there is a record of that telephone call. I lost over $700 just because I could not get a little help from the police, who are supposed to combat crime and help people who ask for assistance, without any kind of discrimination. Years later I discovered that the police station in question was the worst in the city with respect to customer service and how they serve the community - for sure, that kind of behaviour damages the reputation of the whole police force and the city.

Police Do Not Help

Small businesses are often targeted by criminals and dishonest people, who rob in different ways, like asking for credit, stealing merchandise or services paying with fraudulent credit cards, running away without paying for the service received or other means. The thieves know that usually these businesses do not have security, an if an emergency arises and the police are called, they do not show up because they are busy with bigger tasks.

I had a customer who was honest until the day he decided to rob me. He brought his car to my shop to be fixed, and after the general inspection was done, I presented him with an estimate of over $900. He agreed to get the work done and left. When the car was ready, I called him to pick up his car. He soon arrived, ready to pay with a credit card belonging to his uncle. I refused the card because it belonged to somebody else. He insisted saying that his uncle had authorized him to use his credit card and would confirm the payment by phone. It was a dilemma for me because I knew his family, and most of them were my customers.

After begging and reminding me that it was not the first time he had been at the shop, I decided to accept his pleas and asked him for proof that his uncle was aware of the deal; he gave me his uncle's name and telephone number, and when I called, the man on the other end confirmed that he was the owner of the credit card and his nephew could use it. After that conversation I accepted the credit card and called the company for the authorization number. The man signed the copy of the bill and left.

About two months later, I got a letter from the credit card company, telling me that the card used by my customer belonged to a man living in Toronto, who had lost the card and complained about the charge. The company sent me a bunch of papers about the investigation and removed the amount from my account. I called the customer and his uncle but never reached them; I called the company to complain about the authorization they had given me, but they washed their hands of it.

My last resource was the police. I went to the head office, expecting to find polite and educated people who could assist me getting the money owed to me. I explained the case to the person in charge of the office, showing him the papers of the transaction and the ones received from the credit card company. The officer told me that there was nothing they could do and advised me to go to the courts. I did not get any help at all because the officer did not even bother to take the name of the thief who was lose on the streets. I did not follow his advice of going to the courts because of my prior experience. I would lose my money, I already knew that if I win the case in the court, I will lose the money anyway. Once again, I had a bad experience trying to get help from the police. After all those regrettable experiences with the police, I have asked myself many times: What do so many police officers really do in the city? It seems like they not only discriminate against people, but also the service they prove. After 37 years of living in the same city, the attention that I have received from police is ZERO.

Two Police Officers Help a Crook

About twenty years ago, I had the strangest experience of my life. One day I received a customer who explained to me that his car had some kind of problem and he wanted me to take care of it. He showed me a big list of things he wanted fixed; the problems were so many that it seemed he wanted to replace or fix every part in his car. I told him that I had to put the car on the hoist and check everything over to see what the car really needed. He left the car and asked me to call him when I had information about the work needed.

It was obvious that the vehicle did not need everything on the list. I made a new list of the work that needed to be done, which was about 30% of his list. I prepared an estimate an called him; he accepted the information and seemed happy with the whole amount, because it was much less than what he had expected to pay. As soon as he authorized the work, I started working on his car. Before doing any work, I would always tell the customer that if I found something that was not on the estimate I would call before doing that work. I never did anything without the customer's authorization. As I was working on it, I found something that had to be replaced so I called him; I do not remember the exact amount, but including the labour it was less than forty dollars. The customer authorized the extra work and asked me to call him when the job was done.

The next day when I finished the work, I went for a road test and confirmed that everything was working fine. I called the customer and told him that his car was ready for pick up and gave him the exact amount he had to pay. After testing the car, I brought it inside the shop and left the keys on the ignition. Soon after, the customer arrived and asked me what his bill came to. I thought the question was strange as I had told him on the phone the total amount he had to pay; nevertheless, I gave him the information again. He started complaining immediately, saying that I had given him a different amount the day before. I reminded him that I had called about the extra work needed and that he had authorized it. He said that work had been my choice, and he would only pay the amount I had originally quoted him.

We had a pointless discussion, because he was determined not to pay the whole amount, and I was trying to make him understand that we never did anything without the authorization of the customer. Suddenly he left my office without saying anything else.

About forty minutes later, he was back, accompanied by two police officers, one woman and one man. I was surprised to see all of them because I had never experienced any situation like that. The two officers told me that they had a court order saying that I had to give the car to the man and only charge him the original amount. While the officers were showing me the order, the guy went directly to start his car and ran away like a professional thief. I told the officers that they were doing something incorrect, and I also explained to them what had really happened regarding the work done in that vehicle. The officers insisted that they were just complying with the court order. I told them that I did not understand why they were allowing that man to remove a car from my shop without my authorization, as they were supposed to care for the wellbeing of everybody.

We engaged in a useless discussion for a while since the thief was already gone. They insisted that I had the right to go to court to get the money, but I told them that it was obvious to me that the man was not a normal person. It was my first time meeting him, but his attitude was exactly like that of many arrogant people who had a contact, family member, or friend working in a government institution and try to scare everybody else by saying, "Do you know who I am? Do you?"

At the end of the discussion, I told them: "What you have done is enough for me, therefore, I am not going to court for any money, if he refused to pay here what he owes me, there is nothing else I want to do. I am aware that the system supports the illegal behaviour of people who use their contacts to bring two police officers to my shop to enforce something illegal. This is a robbery, and you are complicit in what is clearly a crime. Let's leave everything like it is and forget about the whole thing. You can inform the judge or whoever gave the order to you that I will not claim anything if that is what they are expecting."

Empowered by the Uniform

There was a moment when I was really upset and lost control over my temper because of the injustice of the situation. What that thief did is a huge mystery to me, because ordinary people cannot easily get a court order and be accompanied by two police officers in such a short time. I will never know what happened with the money he owed me, maybe he went to get it for himself right away and perhaps accompanied by the same police officers, who must inform to the court that the order was executed. This was the worst experience I have ever had with the police, and it is one I will never forget.

Now that I am writing this book, I am thinking that those two police officers were prudent and did not treat me the way many people are treated by the police when they try to claim their personal rights, according to the information supplied frequently by the media. I still have the badge numbers of both officers, and I think that they were educated people because they dealt with me patiently without losing their temper. It would have been easy for them to arrest me and charge me with assault and resisting arrest as often happens to people, which would have seen me in jail in addition to losing my money. I suppose those officers are already retired, like myself, but I am sure that if they read this book, they will remember the incident.

There is no doubt that many police officers are respectful, educated, and very patient when dealing with people, but it is also a fact that some of them do not have these qualities; therefore, I hope that my personal experience helps police officers in general to understand that people have the right to submit complaints. And in cases like those discussed later in this book, it is an injustice to take someone's life just because they are trying to explain their point of view. Some police officers do not have the patience or preparation to listen to people and instead use lethal force.

According to the cases investigated and reported in this book, I am sure that many deaths could be avoided if the police officers involved had the professional training to deal with angry people without losing their calm. Obviously, some police officers are so fast to pull the trigger, pepper spray, taser, or any other lethal weapon because they do not have the vocation to be police officers, and those guys, should have never become police officers. This is a profession which requires vocation, preparation, skills, and education. They must NEVER use a weapon to kill a person; a good police officer gains the appreciation, gratitude, admiration, and respect of the people he/she is serving in any community.

WRONGFUL CONVICTIONS

Wrongful convictions have been a significant and concerning issue in this country's legal system for several years, as will be shown with selected examples in this section. Each case, which at the time, caused a fundamental problem in the life of the accused, raised significant issues about the unprofessional ways in which these people were charged and convicted, without appropriate evidence of their involvement in the crimes. Their sagas typically started with the investigators, who in many cases pointed to them (with the approval of the prosecutor) as being the perpetrators of a crime, without any real evidence. These investigators would then mislead the members of the legal system and recruit false witnesses for the trial, fabricate evidence, or hide key information from the defence. The accused would be found guilty of a crime they did not commit and would be sent to prison for years, without any plausible or reasonable way to prove their innocence.

The justice system is great at forgetting about people who have been sent to jail, even if these individuals claim their innocence in the strongest possible ways. The word *justice* is a strong term that means a lot to everybody, to every citizen, without any kind of discrimination, but apparently, not to all officials of the justice system. That word should mean fair treatment, fair application of the law, equal treatment, and impartial treatment of the accused. Whoever oversees the application of the law should ensure that justice is served with integrity and, that officials are honourable and without prejudice. They must be ready to detect and rectify any mistake; always vigilant of the behaviour of those involved in the case, and responsible for the well-being of the accused. This is very important because many people know that there have been cases in which the justice system has been manipulated to the point where innocent people have been wrongfully convicted for crimes they did not commit and have spent decades in jail. In those cases, the officials responsible for the wrongful imprisonment of a person (whether they acted deliberately or were just instruments used to serve the purpose), should be charged and penalized for the committed injustice.

When the justice system does not do a fair job society, in general, is affected. It is contemptible for anyone in a position of authority or within the justice system to damage or destroy the life of a person they know is innocent. That is a crime that should be prosecuted. Unfortunately, as shown in this section, many cases have fallen into this category without any consequences for the actors.

This section highlights some of Canada's most salient cases that have taken place over the last few decades. I share this in the hope of avoiding future wrongful convictions where there is a complicity and impunity of those working in the justice system.

The information presented in these cases has been part of the public domain for years, contained in several news stories, editorials, and other local and national media.

Mother Fights to Prove Her Son's Innocence.

When David, a sixteen-year-old boy from Winnipeg, arrived in Saskatoon one day in January 1969, he never imagined that from that day on, he would be a puppet of the justice system for over twenty-two years, accused by police of a crime that he did not commit.

On the same day as his arrival in that town, somewhere in the city, a nursing assistant was raped and killed. When the police found the body, it was easy for them to charge an unknown teenager who happened to be in the city, accompanied by two other teenagers, minding their own business. David did not take his arrest seriously, since he had not done anything wrong; however, the police officers who took him into custody, wanted personal notoriety, and created an elaborated plan, filled with lies and threats to a selected witness, to get an easy conviction of a young person with no life experience.

To make the plan work before the judicial system, the police officers had the audacity to present a master charge against the accused, and it seems that they had the advice of one of more lawyers in preparing the document to convict this innocent boy. Exactly as planned, David was convicted of the murder of the young woman and sent to jail for the next twenty-two years. That trial was an aberration of the justice system in this country, which has a long list of innocent people paying for crimes they did not commit, such Donald, James, Robert, Anthony, Ivan, Raejean, David, Guy, Romeo, Thomas, Steven, William, and more.

The problem is so rampant that it seems normal in the judicial system to convict innocent people without any concern that some of these wrongly convicted victims spend decades in jail for crimes they did not commit. Once the accused is sent to jail, it appears that nobody cares about them. There have been cases where victims' families have been able to overturn the conviction. It has only been after a long fight with the judicial system, which has remained determined to keep the conviction. In many cases, it hasn't been easy to get the attention of those involved in the trials, as it appears that they do not want to see or hear the truth and are not interested in any opinion other that their own.

Thanks to the fight of his mother and sister against the whole system, David did not rot in jail; they never abandoned him, believing in his innocence. It was obvious that some people with power and working for the government wanted an innocent boy in jail for the rest of his life for a crime that he did not commit. During the trial, the police officers in charge of the case found and prepared witnesses who were willing to offer incriminating evidence against David. These officers' dirty work was successful because their victim was convicted of a crime, they knew he did not commit.

When at last a person can prove their innocence, the legal system refuses to take any blame for the wrong conviction of a person, except that they accept to hold an inquiry to soften the anger of concerned citizens. However, my impression is that the inquiry is good for nothing given that whatever damage has been done, is done, and nobody can undo the injustice. The inquiries usually result in a plethora of recommendations that everybody soon forgets, and they go on making the same mistakes and convicting more innocent people again and again.

Ismon Marroquin

When there is a miscarriage of justice, it is safe to think that officials of the justice system do their part to avoid acknowledging that something went wrong. In David's case, a witness was willing to recant his testimony, which was given under pressure, but the system did not give him the chance for fear of embarrassment. The National Parole Board refused to give David the chance of parole if he did not accept responsibility for the crime. The police, due to their lack of professionalism and ethics decided to present false information during the trial, and the judges refused to consider new evidence to David's benefit; therefore, the accused did not have any chance to prove that a miscarriage of justice had occurred during the trial. The National Parole Board – probably just obeying instructions, insisted that the person applying for parole must take responsibility for the crime of the young woman who was raped and killed. The federal Minister of Justice repeatedly refused to grant any request to correct the injustices made during the trial. That stubborn attitude is an aberration of justice and contempt of the law. The Minister of Justice, as the highest authority in the chain of command, should give every opportunity to the convicted and his lawyers to present all kinds of resources in support of the inmate.

David's lawyer knew the precarious condition that he has in jail, where he was kept in solitary confinement, in a horrible place that inmates called "the hole". With all options closed David and his lawyer decided to apply to the Court of Appeals of Saskatchewan, asking for the judge to hear all the evidence accumulated through the years. At last, after 23 years fighting with the Judicial system and thanks to result of DNA evidence, David was exonerated and cleared of a crime he did not commit. During the 23 years that he was in jail, David suffered of all kinds of abuses on the hands of the judicial system. At the very end, full justice was not done, because everybody who participated in any way in his misery, should go to jail as soon as the result of DNA was known. All of them should be charged for contempt, abuse of authority, negligence, lack of respect for the laws, and cruelty.

The so-called inquiry was yet another sad chapter in David's life, since not only had he suffered in jail for twenty-three years, but he had to relive every step of his long and painful experience. Listening to everyone who could have done something to change the outcome of his wrongful conviction provide inexcusable reasons for acting the way they did, must have been excruciatingly painful. Looking at the faces of every one of his tormentors, while they took turns speaking; the same people who fought so hard to keep him behind bars, must have felt disgusting. Listening to their cynicism, hypocrisy, and shameful attitudes must have been awful.

Personally, I do not believe in inquiries because a lot of recommendations will never relieve the pain that David or any other wrongfully convicted person have felt. I think inquiries are only good for the moment. Nobody learns anything from them, because in a few months or years, another case like this will take place, with other actors or maybe with the same. There have been many wrongfully convicted people in Canada, and those responsible for these convictions are still enjoying their freedom.

The Wrongful Conviction of a Teenager

Donald, an Indigenous teenager from the north, was born in Membertou Reserve in Cape Breton, Sydney, Nova Scotia on September 13, 1953. He was the eldest of thirteen children of Donald Sr and Caroline. On May 28, 1971, he and his friend Sandy were walking together when they crossed paths with two other boys, Roy Ebsary and Jimmy McNeil. Donald and Sandy had the misfortune of being at the wrong place at the wrong time because a confrontation took place, and they were the recipients of racist slurs. Soon after, Sandy was stabbed in the stomach by one of the boys, and Donald was slashed on his arm. Sandy died in the hospital the next day. Donald gave the police a description of the men, but they did not search for the suspects, instead the police decided to arrest and charge Donald for the murder of his friend Sandy, maybe because he was Indigenous and had prior encounters with the local police for minor problems in his community.

Donald never thought that the police would find ways to send him to jail for eleven long years for a crime that he did not commit. However, as reported in later investigations, the police used false witnesses to make sure that Donald would be found guilty of the crime without a reasonable doubt, which would result in a conviction of life in prison. Donald went to trial on November 2, 1971, and was found guilty of murder, he was sentenced to life imprisonment and served almost eleven years of his conviction in the penitentiaries at Dorchester, New Brunswick and Springhill, Nova Scotia. From the biggening, Donald insisted on his innocence. It is unbelievable how the police worked against Donald and sealed his fate for the next eleven years when they knew he was innocent. They prepared and manipulated witnesses and evidence, moreover, ten days after his conviction, Jimmy went to the Sydney police to tell them that an innocent man had been convicted because he had seen Roy stab Sandy. The police, however, dismissed the evidence and considered the case closed. They also hid that evidence from the defense lawyer and the prosecutor in charge of Donald's appeal. Those public servants are dangerous and should be denounced to the respective authorities because they will continue behaving this way as long as they are working as police officers.

In 1982, the RCMP began an investigation into the evidence that Jimmy gave to the Sydney police. During the investigation, the RCMP found defects in the Sydney police department's handling of the case. They had perjured themselves, intimidated witnesses, and withheld Donald's not guilty plea; also, the knife was found in Roy's former residence and it still contained fibres of the clothes Sandy and Donald were wearing the night of the stabbing. With all that evidence, why did the RCMP not charge the police officers who had prepared the case against Donald, knowing that they voluntarily decided to implicate him in a crime that he did not commit? Is this some kind of inter institutional protection?.

Donald was eventually cleared of the crime on appeal and released on parole in March 1982, after spending eleven years in jail. His released came after a witness came forward to say that the killer was somebody else, and it was also due to the good work done by a social justice advocate lawyer. A Royal commission that investigated Donald's wrongful conviction determined that systemic racism was a big factor in the wrongful imprisonment and blamed the police officer, crown lawyers, original defense lawyers, and government officials.

Once he was free, Donald fought for the right of Indigenous people to have free access to fishing and hunting in the entire country. This has been deemed to be Donald's best legacy. In 1983 the Supreme Court of Nova Scotia acquitted Donald of the murder of Sandy.

Mentally Challenged Man Wrongly Accused of Murder

Bryan, a mentally challenged young man, was in jail for one year after being accused of two murders that he did not commit. The police charged him because they said that he had confessed to the crimes, but the young man told them that on the night of the murder, he was in jail. They did not believe him, nor did they bother to investigate or simply check the files. At the end of the shameful affair, the senior crown attorney blamed a clerk for the error, while the defense lawyer blamed the Crown and the police department; the police blamed the incarcerated man for confessing to the crime, and other sources blamed the defense lawyer for trying to make a deal with the prosecutors if his client pled guilty to a lesser charge instead of murder.

If everybody washed their hands like Pilate did, we could say that the game they were playing was ludicrous, because playing tag is fine for little children but not for grown people using the justice system as their playground. No person should be in jail a single day without justification. Considering that the accused was mentally challenged because of fetal alcoholic syndrome, leaving him at the cognitive level of a six-year-old child, he vehemently denied any involvement in the double crime when he was questioned by the police. However eventually he broke down and accepted what police wanted him to say, which is incredible since he was in jail when the crime took place, this confession was convenient for the police, as they could now charge and innocent and mentally challenged man; in the name of the law, empowered by the uniform.

Having Bryan's confession, however, did not prove anything about the crimes. It seems that the poor guy had to memorize a written statement that explained his supposed involvement in the whole affair. Due to his limited learning ability, probably he spent a lot of time with a teacher who helped him memorize what he was supposed to say. When at last he understood his part in the affair, he broke down and cried like a child. The teacher had no idea that Bryan was in jail when the crime took place, and upon learning about this, everything came crashing down. Had it not been for this discovery, Bryan would have spent the rest of his life in jail without anybody caring about his fate.

When a case like this happens for whatever reason, the accused should receive apologies from everyone who participated in the injustice, and the system should compensate the offended with a significant amount of money, although there is no price that can be assigned to humiliation and mental damage resulting from these injustices. Anybody who doubts the depth of this suffering should try it out in their own flesh; only then will they understand. It is outrageous to see the public get upset when a famous, rich, or privileged person with special credentials suffers any kind of humiliation from the judicial system. However, many people turn a blind eye about the suffering of a mentally challenged person. The frequency with which police make these kinds of mistakes is very concerning. Bryan was in jail when the two women were stabbed to death, and without any professional investigation, the police decided to charge that mentally challenged young man because he voluntarily told them that he was the killer. The information published in the media said that initially Bryan vehemently denied any involvement in the crime, however, police prepared him to admit his participation in the crime and the police said that he voluntarily accepted that he was the killer. When the authorities realized that Bryan was in jail the night of the murders, he already had spent a year in jail wrongly incarcerated. The prosecuted dropped all charges against him and the judge declared him a free man and ordered to close the case, but the police never apologized. The whole case against Bryan was an aberration of the justice system because of the deficient investigators. Shame on them.

We Know Who You Are

Thomas, a resident of Vancouver, decided to travel to Winnipeg to visit his daughter one day in December 1981, without imagining that that trip would change his life forever. His arrival and stay in Winnipeg coincided with the murder of Barbara, a beautiful teenager who was killed in her workplace on December 23, 1981. She was strangled with a cord that a witness saw the murderer throw over a bridge into the river. The cord was later recovered by police. According to some witnesses, Thomas looked like the murderer. This resulted in a false accusation, which combined with what appeared to be unprofessional work by local police with the collaboration of the Crown Prosecutor, led to Thomas spending forty-five months in jail.

When the machinery of the justice system works as a whole, there seems to be nothing that can stop it in its track to destroying the life and reputation of a person, and that was exactly what happened to Thomas. In a matter of months, police officers, the chief Crown Prosecutor, witnesses and others moved forward to execute a plan that would calm the population, who were pressing the authorities to find the killer who had been seen by some people inside and outside the donut shop where the girl worked and was murdered. This plan seemed to involve arresting and charging someone as soon as possible and Thomas was the perfect scape goat.

Thomas who had arrived from Vancouver to see his little daughter, was unable to see her because his ex-wife would not let him. He then left a gift for the girl with some relatives and decided to go back to Vancouver. He had to have his car brakes fixed before driving back, so, he stopped at a Canadian Tire store to get the work done. While he was waiting for his car, he got into a conversation with two women who were also waiting for their car to get fixed. He also made a couple of trips to a grocery store close by to pick up candy for sick children, which he later took to four hospitals in the city. During the time he was waiting for his car, somewhere else in the city, the young woman was killed, but Thomas left the city before the crime was discovered.

As he was making his way back to Vancouver, he saw the news of the murder and a picture of the killed girl. Because the young woman looked like a person he knew, he decided to call the police in Winnipeg to inform them that he knew the girl in the picture because she used to babysit a friend's child. The diligent police officers took the telephone call like a confession to the murder, so, instead of thanking the caller, they started framing him as the perpetrator of the crime. When he made the phone call, he did not know that some witnesses had already given information to the police about the killer, whom they described as wearing boots, glasses, and a hat like the one Thomas was wearing. From then on, Thomas started living a personal nightmare. After a short investigation the police arrested and charged him with the murder of the girl. He was in shock and could not believe what was happening to him.

When he was taken in for questioning by police officers working the case, Thomas did not think he would be charged with the crime. He knew he had an alibi. He later denounced the interrogation practices used by the police, saying that during the second interrogation he was the victim of abuse and torture. He was humiliated physically and mentally by two police officers which marked him for ever. They showed no respect for his rights. They were so rude and arrogant that when they charged him, they did not bother to read him his rights nor did they tell him that he had the right to call an attorney and to remain silent in the absence of an attorney. With time, Thomas and his defense lawyer realized that the justice system was determined to make him responsible of the murder, given that they never received crucial information for the defense. Police officers were found to be altering information provided by some of the witnesses, ignoring vital information from another witnesses, and refusing to share information with defense lawyers.

The first trial took place between October and November 1982 and ended in mistrial because the jury could not arrive at a consensus. The second trial took place between February and March 1983 and concluded with a conviction. The Manitoba Court of Appeal overturned the conviction due to multiple errors and ordered a new trial. The third and last trial took place in February 1985 with a conviction for second degree murder. However, the Manitoba Court of Appeal reversed the conviction based on multiple errors and ruled that Thomas could not be tried a fourth time for the same crime. Thomas was acquitted on December 12, 1985. The Supreme Court of Canada did not want to hear a Crown appeal and ordered an end to the prosecution. Thomas was exonerated after spending forty-five months in jail for a crime that he did not commit.

Thomas became physically and mentally sick and never regained the respect that he had in his community because people kept thinking that he was Barbara's murderer. He would even receive anonymous messages from time to time saying: "We know who you are." At the end, he received financial compensation for the time he was incarcerated for a wrongful conviction, but that money will never pay for the destruction of his life. He will be forever a marked and unhappy man thanks to the justice system and the incompetence of the officials who were involved with the case from the very beginning.

Locked in a Cell Twenty-Three Hours a Day

Ivan, was a regular guy who arrived in Vancouver accompanied by his family in the early 1980 from another city where he had a criminal record, including a conviction for attempted rape. After serving his time, he decided to move to British Columbia to start a new life. Around the time he arrived in Vancouver, a serial rapist had raped women living on the first floor of houses or in basement suites. This rapist would assault his victims early in the evenings, threatening them with a knife, so that they would not resist. When police investigated the assaults, they learned that a man with a criminal record was living in the area, therefore, it was easy to pin the blame on Ivan, adding him to a list of wrongfully convicted people in the country. Without any physical evidence, he was arrested and charged with eights counts of sexual assault. He was then convicted, declared a dangerous offender, and locked up indefinitely. He served twenty-seven years in jail for crimes he did not commit.

While he was behind bars, police tried to seal his fate by continuing to add more evidence against him, including a statement from his wife, which police obtained after paying her $1,000, which she gladly accepted as she was on social assistance and was a drug addict. However, one of her daughters later declared that what Ivan's wife had said was not true, explaining that her mother had given that statement to police in exchange for the money she needed for drugs.

During the trial, Ivan did not want to be represented by any lawyer, dismissing three and refusing the assistance of another two. He decided to represent himself because he was confident he would receive justice, as he knew he was innocent. This was a huge mistake, since lawyers know the legal system better than regular citizens. From other stories I have already discussed in this book, we have seen that the prosecution does not always share vital information with the defense, because they do not want to risk losing the case. So, without a lawyer representing him, it became a simple task for the prosecution to prove that he was guilty of the crimes.

The Crown Attorney, on several occasions, did not disclose important information, like the existence of another suspect police officers were investigating and records that the Vancouver police investigators were keeping about a man named Donald, who lived in the same neighbourhood as Ivan as also happened to resemble him. So, when the trial concluded, Ivan was convicted and left to rot in jail like many other wrongfully convicted people in this country. While he was behind bars, similar crimes continued to happen in the same area, which made police think that they may have sent the wrong person to jail. However, it appears that they did not care enough to do anything about it and correct their mistakes, or at least check whether their suspicion was accurate. This seems to be their modus operandi. They preferred to keep an innocent man in jail instead of becoming the focus of an investigation about this wrongful conviction. However, they kept investigating the new cases and soon discovered a man named Robert, who they concluded was the real rapist and serial killer, however, the discovery did not interrupt their sleep.

Justice must be equal for everybody living in a community, even for jail inmates, the system must ensure that there is no abuse while in prison. It is disturbing to hear that Ivan was locked up for many years in solitary confinement for twenty-three hours a day, seven days a week. In a country known for respect of human rights, treating someone like this is an aberration of justice and shameful behaviour, there is no reason or excuse for it. What happened to the justice system? The whole system was either sick, paralyzed or in a coma. Was there no other human being around or close to Ivan, to see what was happening? Was he accused of other crimes that we did not know about? It is a miracle that he did not die or go crazy during this time. When I read about this case and the cruel and barbaric way in which he was treated, I can only think about the inhumane way prisoners in some developing countries have been treated. Some of their stories are narrated in books like One long Night by Andrea Pitzer and the Gestapo by Jacques Delarue. What the authorities did to Ivan while in prison is shameful for the country and disgusting for its citizens. It is obvious that nobody in the justice system respected his constitutional rights.

After Ivan spent almost twenty-seven years in jail, the Court of Appeal reviewed his case and found that there were a lot of errors in the police investigation and during the trial; therefore, it was decided to overturn the conviction and ask for an acquittal in the respective court. With all that information, the Court of Appeal conceded a hearing and acquitted him, but they did not declare him innocent of the charges. The acquittal was based on many factors, mainly that the police and the Crown had hidden important evidence from Ivan before, during, and after the trial. For example, they hid sperm samples, contradictory statements of the victims, and a letter sent by one of the victims to an investigator officer. These errors seemed to follow a systemic pattern with investigators and Crown lawyers across the country. I wonder if these people enjoyed seeing an innocent person disgraced and sent to jail because of their actions.

When superiors in the justice system are aware of this type of cancer within the system and still do nothing to correct the problem, it can only mean that the whole system is rotten. There is no justice in having an innocent man in jail for twenty-seven years when those who participated in his conviction, knowing full well they convicted an innocent man are not prosecuted and sent to jail. Are we all accomplices of that impunity? Those people are the real criminals, and if the whole system knows it and does not prosecute them, our justice system is in huge trouble.

In 2015 the Supreme Court of Canada approved compensation for this case. Since then, Ivan has sued the different levels of government that had something to do with his conviction. The British Columbia Supreme Court stated that Ivan should receive up to $43 millions in compensation. That opinion infuriated the corrupt prosecution lawyers, whose disgusting reaction shows that they only care about the money and not the justice. A person went to jail for twenty-seven years for a crime he never committed. He was in solitary confinement for many years, only able to see the light of day for one hour each day. However, this does not seem to matter to those lawyers and case workers. They obviously do not care about the feelings of the person whose life was destroyed with their knowledge and collusion, those lawyers should be ashamed of their conduct because they are supposed to give their best to ensure a fair trial and that justice is served, no matter whose side they represent. Hiding vital information that can help the cause of a wrongly convicted person is a crime that should be on their shoulders forever.

About the dramatic and ridiculous reaction of the prosecutor lawyers and based on the known damage that they caused on purpose, I, as a simple citizen respectfully ask the Supreme Court to impose a more impartial and fair decision. Order a compensation to Ivan for $43 million by the lawyers and justice officials who resulted responsible for the injustice committed, but that money should come from their own pockets, not from taxpayers' money. Moreover, each of them should be sentenced to five years in jail under the same conditions that Ivan experienced. In addition, the association of professionals must put each of them on a professional trial to make them responsible of their unprofessional conduct for knowingly convicting an innocent man to a long time in jail.

People do not need special qualifications to realize that in Ivan's case the prosecutors did the worst of their instincts in making sure that they were convicting an innocent man, nobody can understand their personal reasons, but they were perverse and maybe with diabolic attitude.

Common sense tells us that law professionals should be responsible for keeping the justice in a high pedestal to be seen by every citizen and never use it to comply with perverse purposes against any citizen; whoever do not do that should be prosecuted. It is time to take action to see the splendour of a clean justice system.

A Miscarriage of Justice

James is another victim on the long list of wrongly convicted people by the justice system. In 1991 he was convicted of first-degree murder for the death of his friend and partner in business, Perry. James and Perry were partners in a business that consisted of stealing, dismantling, and selling car parts. In 1989, the police discovered the chop shop and searched the place. They found enough evidence to arrest both friends and charge them with multiple criminal offences, including possession of stolen property. During the initial investigation, prosecutors and police decided to make a deal with Perry, offering to reduce his sentence to two or three years if he testified against James. Perry accepted the deal but did not show up on the court date when the agreement was to be confirmed. The offer of a deal was withdrawn, and police started looking for Perry. Eventually, the charges against James were dropped since the police were not able to find Perry.

After three months, Perry's body was discovered with two shots in his chest. The officers in charge of the investigation immediately assumed that the murderer was James who was trying to stop Perry's confession in court. Therefore, without any evidence, the investigators arrested and charged James with first degree murder.

To get a conviction, the prosecution and police decided to prepare a case against James. They paid two career criminals for their testimony against James and prepared them to say that James told them he was planning to kill Perry to prevent him from testifying in court against him. The only evidence that the prosecution had against James were three hairs found in his van, which police and the prosecution were sure belonged to Perry. The police and the prosecution argued that James had gotten into a struggle with Perry when trying to take him to the murder place, and during the struggle Perry left the hairs in the van.

During the trial, the Crown Prosecutor, known for his merciless and almost criminal attitude against the accused, and the police officers involved in the case, used the two false witnesses to testify in front of the jury against James. The two men did the dirty job exactly as they were instructed, and the three hairs found in James's van were also added as forensic evidence and critical evidence, however none of that was shared with the defense lawyer. Therefore, the accused did not have a chance to prove his innocence. He was totally at the mercy of the prosecution, led by a corrupt lawyer. The plan appeared to work, since the jury considered that the evidence presented by the prosecution was compelling. With a strong case against the accused, on June 14, 1991, the jury convicted James of first-degree murder for the death of his friend and business partner Perry. He was sentenced to life without the chance of parole for twenty-five years.

Another innocent person was added to the long list of wrongfully convicted people in the country. Fortunately for James the death penalty does not apply in this country; otherwise, he and many others who have been wrongfully convicted, would have faced death due to a corrupt Crown Prosecutor in the justice system. Evidently, this was a miscarriage of justice. James appealed the conviction but was denied in December 1992 by the Manitoba Court of Appeal. He spent the next twelve years in jail until the miscarriage of justice was discovered.

With the help of the Association in Defense of the Wrongfully Convicted, James got the evidence he needed to review his conviction. In December 2002, Innocence Canada used DNA tests that proved the three hairs presented to the jury, did not belong to Perry but to three different people. Furthermore, the defense lawyers and the lawyers for the Association in Defense of the wrongfully convicted revealed problematic testimony of witnesses and that the prosecution, through the police, had paid large amounts of money to the key witnesses against James. They proved that the two stellar witnesses received a huge amount of money – one of them alone getting $83,000 plus immunity from a Saskatchewan arson charge. It was clear that for the plan to succeed, the police and the prosecutor had taken extraordinary steps to keep the defense in the dark throughout the case by not sharing any information about the preparation of false witnesses, false evidence, granting of immunity to witnesses, distortion of events, gaining the support of the public through lies, and more.

It is hard to understand why someone like the Crown prosecutor would behave in such an unethical manner, particularly given his influence over the outcome of key cases where people's lives were at stake. However, based on the many published cases over the years, it is likely that this was his modus operandi, and nobody was aware of his unethical behaviour. Maybe everyone was an accomplice, turning a blind eye to every injustice committed by him until his cruelty and disregard for the wrongfully convicted was discovered. Besides James's case, he put his mark on the wrongful convictions of three other Manitobans, who were also wrongfully convicted.

In 2005 the Minister of Justice and Attorney General of Canada overturned James's conviction and stayed the charges. James was awarded over $4 million in compensation for the thirteen years that he spent in jail for a crime he did not commit. In the same year the government of Manitoba called for a public inquiry, to get more of the same – recommendations that are not implemented.

His Word Against History

Steven was only fourteen years old when he was sentenced to death by hanging, accused of a crime that he did not commit. Without any proof he was accused of raping and killing his classmate, Lynne. On June 9, 1959, Steven gave a ride to Lynne in his bicycle to the intersection of County Road and Highway 8, close to the town of Clinton, Ontario. After he dropped her off and she got on her way by foot, he started riding back toward the school. When he was crossing the bridge over the Bayfield River, he stopped to take a last look at his friend, and it was then that he saw her getting into a grey Chevrolet with a yellow licence plate; by the colour of the plate, he knew that the vehicle was not local. He assumed that she knew the driver as it appeared that she was willingly getting into the car. Many people had seen Steven with Lynne sitting on the bicycle and when he was alone on the bridge looking back at Lynne. Others had seen him crossing the bridge and later in the afternoon at the school. Unfortunately, that short ride almost cost him his life, and while he was not put to death, he practically lost his life because of the trauma and mental and physical suffering he endured for fifty years for a crime that he did not commit.

Lynne never got home that night, so, her father reported her missing. Lots of people helped with the search, and her body was found within two days. When she was found she was semi-naked. She had been raped and strangled with her blouse in a bushy area on the property of a twenty-five year-old man named Bob Lawson, close to the place where she was last seen by Steven getting into the vehicle. According to Bob, he saw a car near his fence and went to report it to the Royal Canadian Airforce; however, he claimed that the on-duty officer did not pay attention to the information he was providing.

While many of the stories discussed in this book show the horrible consequences of the justice system failures that resulted in wrongful convictions, I would say that this case is by far one of the worst, as it is filled with injustices and what appears to be significant collusion to condemn a child for a crime, he did not commit. It was obvious that the justice system was in a hurry to find a culprit for the crime, and it decided that Steven was the one to blame, mainly because he was the last one to see Lynne alive. Two days after Lynne's body was found, the police investigating the case, led by inspector Harold, arrested, and charged Steven with the rape and murder of his friend. They had no case because there was no physical proof of any wrongdoing by Steven, except that the police found some lacerations on his penis, which still did not prove anything. But because the investigators were not willing to let go their theory that Steven was the perpetrator, the case was forced through the system, and Steven was sentenced to death by hanging based on a trial that lasted only two weeks.

While Steven was waiting to be hanged, the government decided to change his sentence to life in prison, which gave him a chance to appeal. However, every single appeal, was rejected by every court, including the supreme court, despite there never being any proof about his guilt beyond a reasonable doubt. The entire case was a disaster and suspicious, as nobody took time to think twice about the consequences of sending a child to a penitentiary for life, specially without any forensic evidence. The whole case seemed like a science fiction novel and not something based on real life. Nobody lifted a finger to evaluate the reasonableness of what was happening; not the courts, the lawyers, the witness or the public. Instead, everybody seemed to be hypnotized against a child whose crime was to have been friends with another child who had been the victim of rape and murder by a psychopath who was still on the lose and who was not at risk of being caught because the police and the justice system were satisfied with their incompetent work to hang an innocent child.

One does not have to be a genius or have a doctorate in criminology to see that Steven's case was a deliberate miscarriage of justice right from the start. Common sense would say that if there is not a single piece of evidence, the case is weak. There were many reasons to be suspicious about the handling of this case, since everyone involved was more interested in proving that they had the right person in prison, than applying the law to find the killer. The lead investigator refused to investigate other possible suspects, of which there were at least three. One of them was Airforce Alexander, who was a heavy drinker with a history of sexual offenses and who lived twenty minutes from the place of the murder. Another possible suspect was a man who had previously been convicted of rape and who was working casually as an electrician at the base; moreover, he knew Lynne and her family, which made him the strongest suspect. Lynne seemed to know the driver of the vehicle she got into. The last possible suspect was Larry, a salesman who had a Chevrolet 1957 similar to the one Steven saw when Lynne was getting into the vehicle. The police had their man in jail and were not interested in looking for anybody else.

The police investigating the case charged Steven the same day they arrested and interviewed him, and the charge was rape and murder without any physical evidence. The prosecutor was satisfied with the charges and not only supported that decision, but also ordered that the accused, a child, be tried as an adult. To strengthen the case against Steven, the prosecutor created his own version of events by claiming that Steven and Lynne had never crossed the bridge but had left the road before getting to the bridge. Once off the road, he had taken her into a bush, raped her, and killed her. The prosecutor, however, never explained why Steven did not show any signs that proved Lynne had fought for her life. He also dismissed all claims from the children who said they had seen Steven alone on the bridge with his bicycle nor did he share any important documents with the defense. After everything was over, he refused to give any interviews to the media.

Several children were manipulated to say certain things that would help the prosecution; however, one child later shared that what she said in court was not the same as what she said when she was interviewed. Another child said that he was confused because somebody had asked him to talk to Bob, the owner of the property where Lynne's body was found, so that his statements would match the star witness's statement. In addition to the claims made by these children, Steven shared that while in jail, he was drugged with LSD and truth serum, so that he could give a confession to the crime.

The doctor who conducted Lynne's autopsy provided various possibilities about the time when Lynne was killed, and one of the possibilities was between 7:00 and 7:45 PM, which is the time when Lynne and Steven were together. This was the statement the prosecutor decided to use against Steven, disregarding everything else the doctor had said. The jury concluded, based on witness statements, that Steven was guilty but recommended mercy for him. However, the judge sentenced him to death by hanging. Steven appealed the conviction when his sentence was changed to life in prison, but he was never successful.

When he was eighteen years old, he was transferred to Collins Bay penitentiary in Kingston, Ontario, and after ten years in jail he applied for parole. He was released and changed his name to Steven Bowers to start a new life working as a millwright and living in the house of his parole officer. He started a new life, got a job, got married, and had three children.

In 1997, Innocence Canada decided to take part in the legal fight to demonstrate that Steven was wrongly convicted. Its support, in conjunction with the Fifth State television program, gave many people the opportunity to think back to the 1959 crime and share their views that Steven paid for a crime he did not commit, and that the real criminal could be among the citizens of their community. In 2007, almost fifty years after he was sent to jail, the Ontario Court of Appeal overturned his conviction, declaring the case a miscarriage of justice, but the same court refused to declare him innocent of the crime. This means that he remains a suspect to many people, specially to Lynne's family, who think that he is guilty of the rape and murder of their daughter.

In 2008 Steven was awarded $6.5 million by the Ontario Government as compensation for the time he spent in jail waiting to be executed for a crime that he did not commit.

Judicial Monstrosity

Wilbert was a Canadian prospector born in 1915 in the town of Gaspe, which was in a mountainous region of Quebec. He enjoyed the woods, so much that as soon as he had the chance, he built a cabin there, where he spent most of his life. With time, people in the region knew him as the woodsman. He made a living as a guide for hunters looking for bears, geese, ducks, and other animals, as well as for fishers looking for special places to fish. His cabin was located strategically to serve hunters from different places, specially from the United States, where there was an association with over 200,000 members, many of whom liked to go to Quebec for bear hunting, a sport that was attracting many tourists every year, which brought lots of revenue to different places in the province.

Empowered by the Uniform

Wilbert had a common-law partner, Marion Petrie, with whom he fathered a child they named James. According to people who knew Wilbert, he was a nice, polite, and peaceful man who never got into trouble, and he always helped people who needed him. In 1953 a group of hunters from Pennsylvania went to Quebec to hunt bears. Wilbert came across them when their truck broke down and they were stuck in the woods, so, he offered to take one of them to town to get a fuel pump for the truck. After that, they went their separate ways, but he promised to check in on them a few days later. When he did, he found the truck, but there was nobody there. He waited a few hours, but when nobody came back, he left, the three Americans hunters had disappeared, and nobody was able to give any information about them. People thought that maybe they were deep into the bush, but when time passed without any sight of them, a formal investigation was initiated. One month after their disappearance, their bodies were found in the woods. The bodies had been eaten by wild animals; all of them had gun shots wounds, and pockets on their clothes were turned inside out, meaning they had been killed by someone who saw them in the bush and had decided to kill and rob them.

At that time, the Premier of Quebec was Maurice Duplessis, a corrupt individual, capable of doing anything illegal to get what he wanted. Everybody knew that his name was synonymous with corruption, given the tactics he used to win the election. Running for the Union National Party, he would provide small appliances, liquor, money, and food to voters to beat the Liberal Party candidate. While the strategy was not legal, the result was excellent because he won the election and set a new way of running provincial government based on corruption.

Because hunting was a significant source of revenue for the province, this news was problematic. The case was so important that the Secretary of State of the United States personally called the premier to ask him to investigate the murder as soon as possible, and the premier, knowing that these murders would jeopardize their reputation and business in general, promised to solve the crimes quickly. He assured the Secretary that those responsible would be brough to justice. Since he was a corrupt individual, he knew how to bend the law and use it to his own benefit, so, he decided to give the life of an innocent man from Gaspe, Quebec in exchange for the money of an American Club of 200,000 hunters.

Maurice Duplessis was also the chief prosecutor of Quebec; therefore, it would not be difficult for him to get a conviction for the selected man. He sent a carefully selected group of people to Gaspe to investigate the crime. These includes Alphonse Matte, Quebec's chief of detectives, who was known to be the cruelest police officer in the province, and two top prosecutors. These three men were, without a doubt, the best to do the dirty work the premier needed done so that an innocent man could be accused. They were sent with the mission of finding a perpetrator at any cost. That mission was not difficult because it was well known that a man lived in the woods, whom everybody called the woodsman. The investigators decided that he would be a perfect target. Who else would be a better candidate than him? So, he was hand picked.

The next step was just a matter of preparing a credible case and then, arresting and charging the innocent man, who was minding his own business and had no idea he would be the perfect scapegoat to save the economy of a province led by a corrupt premier. The investigators were able to comply with their mission without a problem, as there was nothing to investigate. The perfect candidate was arrested and charged with one of the three murders, as the law did not allow for more than one charge for the same type per trial. The woodsman was convicted and sentenced to death by hanging for a crime he did not commit. To make everything appear fair, the premier also selected a lawyer who had been one of his campaign supporters – an irresponsible and unreliable alcoholic – to represent Wilbert during the trial. Surely this was done as payback for the help he had received during his campaign, or maybe the premier wanted to ensure that Wilbert would have no chance of survival after the trial. The show was complete when a jury was selected to confirm what was already decided by the premier and his accomplices…to hang an innocent man. It appeared that the jury had the mission of delivering a guilty verdict to comply with the premier's instructions who had the responsibility to please the American organization of hunters.

The case was easy for the prosecution because Wilfred spoke only English, and the trial was conducted in French. It took only thirty minutes of deliberations for the jury, to find Wilbert guilty of murder. Incredibly, the jury treated the case with such coldness that the members were discussing the town's anniversary while deliberating on the fate of a man, who would die even with no evidence of physical proof against him. After the conviction Wilfred appealed to the Quebec Court of Appeal, but his request was denied. The same thing happened when he appealed to the Supreme Court of Canada. It is absolutely unbelievable that such a judicial monstrosity took place with total impunity in a country championing human rights around the world. The corruption of one man, tinted and corrupted the whole system for ever. Shame on everyone who had something to say or do with this juridic monstrosity.

The premier's last pleasure of his legacy was denying Wilfred his last wish, to marry his common-law partner. She begged for permission to marry Wilfred, but the premier denied the request. The defense lawyer appointed by the premier did his job exactly like expected; he was completely incompetent, drunk during the whole trial and failed to supply any witnesses, despite promising that he would present at least one hundred during the trial.

At the end of the political show and the caricature of trial, Wilfred, the innocent woodsman was hanged at the Montreal Bordeaux Prison on February 10, 1956, at 12:01 A.M. On that day and time, a dark page was written on the Canadian judicial system.

In 2006, Philippe Cabot confessed to his family that he had killed the three American hunters from Pennsylvania with his own son as a witness. However, no authority has been interested to investigate this horrendous crime against an innocent man who was hanged in the name of the law. That aberration of justice will not be forgotten.

A Wrongful Conviction Is the Easiest Way to Destroy a Life

Robert, a twenty-four-year-old man, and Elizabeth, a twenty-two-year-old woman, had been talking about getting married once the circumstances were appropriate; however, everything ended on June 19, 1990, when Elizabeth disappeared after going to the University campus. The couple had met at the University of Toronto, and when Elizabeth went missing, she was still a student, while Robert had already graduated with a degree in physiology. When Elizabeth did not show up at home, a search team was organized. Only her car was found, with her blood on the back seat, which assured everybody that something terribly wrong had happened to her. The police started the investigation, but right from the start they thought that her boyfriend was responsible for the crime. Robert was interviewed for many hours, but he denied any involvement in her disappearance; police let him go but kept him as the only suspect.

Nowadays not many people are surprised to hear the news that somebody spent many years in jail accused of a crime they did not commit, and the worst is that instead of fixing the problem, those in charge of the justice system do things that continue to cause its deterioration. This may be because nobody is really interested in fixing the many problems, so, in a way they enable the atrocities that for years have resulted in several wrongful convictions. Unfortunately for Robert, almost everyone involved in the case contributed to his wrongful conviction, destroying his future forever. Not only was he already grieving the loss of his girlfriend, but the system subjected him to additional pain resulting in the loss of his freedom. Once the damage is done and the court of public opinion has convicted someone, there is no way to reverse that conviction, even if the justice system says something different years later. It is easy to ruin or destroy a person's reputation, but it takes a lifetime to rebuild it.

Following the police investigation, the Toronto police charged Robert with murder and arrested him on November 19, 1990, exactly five months after Elizabeth went missing. As the investigation was proceeding, it became known that one of the detectives investigating the case was preparing a special report to make sure Robert would be found guilty by the jury. The officer's corrupt approach inflicted a lot of damage on an innocent man who had had nothing to do with the disappearance of his girlfriend. That shameful and corrupt behaviour was supported by the lawyer in charge of the prosecution, who had known the couple from before. It appeared that he was jealous of Robert, since Elizabeth had ended her romantic relationship with him before starting to date Robert.

Both the police and the Crown prepared false witnesses, and because they needed certainty that these witnesses would follow through with the plan, they decided to hypnotize them to improve their memory and ensure they would do well during the trial. During the trial, the two-star witnesses were hesitant when providing their statements. One of them said that she saw Robert and Elizabeth at a picnic table the day Elizabeth disappeared, but later she was no longer sure about having seen them. The other witness said that he saw a man driving Elizabeth's car three days after she disappeared, but he was not sure who was driving the car. Given the lack of reliable information provided by these witnesses, the judge instructed the jury to rely on the prosecutor's statements before they went into deliberations. This was wrong on many levels. The judge should have only instructed the jury in an impartial way. In addition, it was known that the prosecutor and the police had withheld critical information from the defense, which could have been used to help prove Robert's innocence. Once again, a jury found an innocent defendant guilty of first-degree murder, and he was sentenced to life in prison. Weeks later, the conviction was downgraded to second degree murder, but the sentence remained unchanged. Parole was not an option for seventeen years.

While Robert was in jail, he learned about Innocence Canada and contacted them immediately. A lawyer with the organization took the case and soon realized that it was plagued with errors, hence providing an opportunity to appeal and get Robert out of prison on bail. The appeal was presented to the Toronto Court of Appeal, and Robert was released on bail on March 31, 2000.

After serving eight years in jail for a murder he did not commit, the Court of Appeal determined that Robert's trial had been unfair because it contained many errors. They ordered a new trial in 2004. When everything was ready for the new trial to start, the prosecution decided there were no real witnesses that could be called for the second trial and rested the case; therefore, Robert was acquitted on April 22, 2008, eighteen years after his wrongful conviction.

This was another wrongful conviction that destroyed the life of an innocent young man, who will carry the stigma of the conviction for the rest of his life. Many people, possibly even his close friends and family, may have doubts about his innocence. The damage done by the police and the prosecutor to Robert's reputation will be hard to correct for the rest of his life. Sometimes in the justice system the real crooks are free of prosecution; they are prosecution lawyers, police detectives, and false witnesses who lend themselves to manipulation. And the worst part is that the real perpetrator of the crime is free somewhere.

The Power of DNA

Guy Paul, a twenty-four-year-old factory worker, lived in Quenneville, Ontario, next door to Christine, a nine-year-old girl who disappeared on October 3, 1984. After a large search, her decomposed remains were found on a farm on December 31, 1984. With brutal evidence of sexual assault and stabs wounds. After the girl remains were found, the police collected evidence found in the body, especially semen, which was tested in a laboratory. However, since DNA testing was still a very new technology, no real readings were obtained. Another test was done, but the result was similar.

The police were interested in one person as the main suspect; he had been selected from the start of the investigation as the perpetrator of the crime. This person was the next-door neighbour. With that mission in mind, the investigators began to manipulate Christine's mother and brother, asking them to adjust the time of disappearance in such a way that their neighbour could have been at his home when the school bus dropped off the girl at home. Guy Paul was still at work at that time, and after leaving work, he had stopped to buy groceries, so the time when the girl was abducted did not match the time when Guy Paul got home.

The day Christine went missing, her mother got home and found that the girl was not there, but her school bag was on the counter, which proved that she had been inside the home for a while. Guy Paul did not help in the search, nor did he attend the girl's funeral. Police thought this was suspicious behaviour, so, on April 22, 1985, Guy Paul was arrested and charged with first degree murder, without any physical or real evidence. He was denied bail and sent to jail for ten months, during which time police and prosecutors made a deal with two inmates, asking them to try to get a confession from Guy Paul. But he never admitted to killing Christine. In addition, an undercover police officer was also in jail to get a confession from him, which he also never got. However, during the trial, all three testified that he had confessed to them that he was the killer. These confessions were added to the grotesque picture the two prosecutors painted of Guy Paul as a sexual predator, hungry to get the girl next door. They based this description on a hair found in his car and some clothing fibres they had collected somewhere around the houses.

Guy Paul was acquitted on February 7, 1986, but the acquittal was met with strong criticism from the police, the media, and Christine's family, since everybody was now sure Guy Paul was guilty. Therefore, the Attorney General of Ontario made a successful appeal to the Supreme Court, so, on November 17, 1988, the Supreme Court dismissed the acquittal on the ground that the trial judge has given confusing instructions to the jury.

At the second trial, Guy Paul's defense lawyers asked for disclosure of the police reports that had not been given to the defense during the first trial. Lots of useful information was obtained by the defense, including information that proved that the investigators had fabricated the case against Guy Paul. However, the jury found Guy Paul guilty of first-degree murder on June 30, 1992, but fortunately, because of a third DNA test that proved somebody else was Christine's killer, after only a few weeks of his conviction he was released on bail on February 9, 1993. Scientists at a Boston laboratory, using advance technology, were able to obtain a DNA reading that was different from Guy Paul's DNA, which proved that he was innocent of Christine's murder.

The pattern of a wrongful conviction usually starts right from the very beginning of the investigation when detectives handpick a potential guilty person without taking the time to look for other possible suspects. The whole case is prepared around the initial work of the detectives, who collude with the prosecution lawyers to prepare a sophisticated spiderweb of events, including the coaching of potential witnesses, manipulation of evidence, selection and instruction of the jury, and information released to the media. The problem is repetitive around the country, almost with the same errors, and the situation is so common that in the end nobody feels responsible, ashamed, or remorseful about having been involved in yet another wrongful conviction. This pattern is expected to continue until the system decides to punish or discipline all those involved in these colossal miscarriages of justice.

Guy Paul received a public apology from the authorities and compensation of $1.25 million. He bought a property north of Toronto, got married and now has two Children. In 2020 Toronto police were able to identify Christine's killer using DNA. The killer was Calvin Hoover a close family friend, who had kept visiting the family after the murder. He had committed suicide in 2015.

Man, Wrongfully Convicted of Killing His Wife

Ronald, a thirty-two year old man, married with three children, was a person with a clean record and living a happy life as a bank manager in Prince Edward Island, until the day when his wife, Brenda, chocked at home while eating cereal on August 16, 1986. She was taken to hospital, where a young and inexperienced doctor working in the emergency room intubated her incorrectly, provoking immediate death. The next day a pathologist without forensic training performed an autopsy but could not find the cause of death, except for a scratch inside her throat. Due to his inexperience, and the fact that he had to submit the autopsy results, he had the great idea of saying that she had died by strangulation, a statement that undoubtedly condemned her husband to jail.

Without conducting a proper investigation, police officers arrested Ronald and charged him with second degree murder. It is regrettable that there are many cases of innocent people in jail because the police did not take the time or have the willingness to properly investigate the cases before pressing charges; and this is one of those cases where the negligence of police officers put an innocent man behind bars. If police did not bother to do a careful or professional investigation, the justice system once again convicted an innocent man for a crime he did not commit. With a little more investigation, or with expert professionals at the hospital, where Ronald's fate was decided, a shameful ending would have been avoided. Common sense would say that when the life of somebody is on the line of fire, whoever is investigating the case should be careful with the handling of critical information – if anybody has to go to jail for Brenda's death, it is safe to say that the inexperienced doctor who intubated the woman and the pathologist without forensic training should be the ones.

Ronald immediately appealed his conviction to the Newfoundland Appeal Court and waited in jail, hoping that the result would come in a reasonable time and clear him of any responsibility in the death of his wife; however, to the surprise of Ronald and everybody else following the case, time passed without any decision from the Court of Appeal for years. In an aberration of justice, the appeal was heard by the Newfoundland Appeal Court until 1998, ten years later, a real calamity. People with common sense do not excuse that kind of errors, or better yet, that kind of irresponsible behavior of the members of the court. People without any professional background understand that the attitude of the court was irresponsible, negligent, and with extreme lack of respect for the inmate, the public, and the laws. The lawyers waited for the conclusion without moving a finger, which shows the carelessness and lack of interest the justice system has put in the life of people doing time in jail, especially when there are inmates wrongfully convicted waiting for decisions of the court. Shamefully, ten years after the appeal, the Newfoundland Court of Appeal put aside the conviction of second-degree murder and ordered a new trial.

At the Supreme Court trial, the defense presented two professional witnesses with vast experience in their field as forensic pathologists. Both testified that Brenda could not have died as a result of strangulation but from panic, which altered the normal functioning of the organs, resulting in heart failure. The defense successfully argued that their client was arrested before the autopsy was done, which was illegal and suspicious. However, the prosecution kept insisting that the cause of death was strangulation and presented expert witnesses, but after five months of deliberation and evidence, the jury declared that Ronald was innocent of the crime for which he had been accused and jailed for eight years. He was acquitted on June 29, 2000.

The damage done to Ronald was huge and unnecessary, and it could have been avoided if the two people who attended Brenda at the hospital had enough experience or the integrity to say that they were not prepared to attend that kind of emergency. Both were incompetent and should not have been there at all. Along with this, the investigators should have done a better job investigating the case.

Ronald lost the opportunity to see his children grow up and be part of those precious years of their lives. If the justice system worked fairly, it would not tolerate long delays by the courts to deal with applications that are part of their normal responsibilities. Waiting ten years to resolve an appeal is an aberration of justice and a shameful discredit to the system, because the lives of people depend on those applications. There is no excuse to wait so long; it is an abuse of power and a matter of professional arrogance. The lives of others deserve respect, especially if they are deprived of their rights and freedom.

Ronald called for an inquiry into his wrongful conviction, and consequently the Government of Newfoundland and Labrador paid $750,000 in compensation for the eight years he spent in jail and for the unprofessional way in which his case was treated from the moment his wife arrived at the hospital. There are no excuses for the members of the appeal's court to have extremely important document hidden in a bunch of papers for ten years while the affected person rotted in jail for a crime he did not commit. It is unbelievably that nobody moved a finger during such a long period of time. If it was negligence, those people do not deserve to be part of an important judicial institution, but if it was deliberate, those people committed a crime and should be prosecuted like anybody else, because no person is above the law.

The amount of money handed to Ronald to keep him quiet is ridiculous after the government sent him to spend ten years of his life behind bars, accused of a crime he did not commit. The compensation given to him seems to be an ugly joke; it is like adding insult to his injury or saying to him: "hey you, this money is what your life is worth". The justice system humiliated and destroyed the life of that innocent man. Many public servants were playing with the life of Roland for ten years, since the moment he was arrested, until the moment he recovered his freedom. When this kind of mistakes or crimes are left unpunished, the normal and simple citizens perceive everywhere nauseating odors, and that is a sign that the whole system is getting rotten.

A Wrongful Conviction from a Perverse Investigation

Glen was convicted of the murder of his girlfriend, Brenda, who was a well-known prostitute on the streets of Halifax. On November 12, 1995, somebody killed her and left her body in a parking lot, where police started the murder investigation. Right from the start and without any hesitation, police wrongly concluded that Glen was her killer, and they did not bother to look for other possible suspects, even when they knew there were two sex predators in the area. They arrested and charged Glen in 1998 with first degree murder. Glen was convicted and sent to jail for seventeen years for a crime he did not commit, according to extensive evidence collected while he was in jail.

It is possible that the police acted in bad faith against Glen, because despite knowing of another potential suspects, they decided to build a case against Glen, recruiting false witnesses and basing their case of his romantic relationship with Brenda. The trial took place in 1999 and an innocent man was sent to jail, while the real killer was never investigated for reasons only known to police. To arrest and charge Glen with Brenda's murder, the Nova Scotia police colluded with the RCMP, which was discovered during the private and impartial investigation that took place when Innocence Canada and the media showed interest in discovering the truth to help this innocent man.

In 1996, following Brenda's murder, Glen moved to British Columbia from Halifax. Unfortunately, he did not know that police officers in charge of Brenda's murder investigation were trying to build a monumental case against him by using several people with bad reputations, who in return for their statements received compensation promises. Margaret, another prostitute, told police officers that Glen had raped her, and during his actions he confessed to her that he had killed Brenda. But after some time, she changed her confession, blaming a serial killer for her rape, someone who was not a suspect in Brenda's murder. Margaret was then arrested several times for misdemeanours until she agreed to testify against Glen.

Another witness was a drug addict and Glen's nephew, whom to gain police trust, told investigators that in a conversation with his uncle, he had confessed that he had killed Brenda. To complete the colourful list of witnesses, the investigators obtained statements from two jailhouse residents, who voluntarily told police that Glen had confessed to them that he was the person who had killed Brenda. It was obvious to everybody that the Halifax regional police and the RCMP did not conduct a proper investigation, and it seemed like they were so interested in convicting Glen that they refused to consider another possible suspect. Because of those errors Brenda's murder has not been solved after twenty-five years.

A Newfoundland lawyer hired a private investigator, a retired RCMP officer, who immediately found discrepancies in the testimonies of the Crown witnesses, especially in the time frame related to the murder. One witness said that Glen confessed to murdering Brenda at 4:15 AM, while another said that he saw Brenda alive at 5:00 AM. The private investigator gave his finding to the Chief of the Halifax Police Department and to the lawyers prosecuting the case, assuring them that according to the investigation, Glen had not killed Brenda. But in a strange and suspicious decision, they dismissed the findings. Glen fought against the system but lost his appeal in 2006.

In 2003, Dave, a profiler officer with the RCMP, had the impression that Glen was not responsible for the murder and decided to conduct a personal investigation, which was not viewed positively by his coworkers and superiors in the organization. His analysis gave enough information to point to a serial killer as Brenda's killer. According to his findings, the evidence collected would be enough to overturn Glen's conviction. However, while he was investigating the case, his superiors told him that he was wasting his time, and after that he received a direct order from his RCMP superiors to stop investigating that case.

When Dave finished his investigation, he was supposed to give the file to the defense, but he made the mistake of giving it to the Violent Crime Linkage Analysis system (VICLAS) of the RCMP. After that, he took two weeks of holidays and when he came back to work, he realized that his office had been ransacked and the file containing the results of his investigation had been erased and destroyed. He was also transferred to another locations. He learned that the file had been destroyed by order of the authorities of the RCMP. This eliminated evidence and vital information that would overturn Glen's conviction.

Glen spent the next ten years in jail, during which time he was assaulted many times by inmates and even by guards at Dorchester Penitentiary. He was tortured by those who were supposed to keep him safe. He developed a mental illness, suffered multiple heart attacks, and a beating that resulted in a broken leg. That disgusting attitude of the RCMP was not accidental. It is possible that some of their officers had a special interest in a big cover up, trying to keep Glen in jail forever and protecting the real killer.

It is very concerning when a prestigious institution like the RCMP, violates basic human rights keeping Glen in jail maliciously and knowing that he was innocent of the crime. That case should have been investigated by senior authorities to punish whoever was responsible for that inappropriate behaviour inside the organization; however, nobody did anything about it. Somebody must have been held accountable for the decision to do something this malicious to an innocent man. Whoever destroyed the file was trying to protect criminals in the city; maybe these criminals were paying for protection, or they knew something about the activities of these police officers and were blackmailing them.

After losing his appeal in 2006, Glen received the help and legal assistance of Innocence Canada, an organization that took his case to the federal Department of Justice Criminal Conviction Review group, where the case was investigated by a lawyer who concluded that a miscarriage of justice had probably occurred. The defense lawyer asked the Crown to disclose the information in possession of the RCMP, but the request was ignored. It was obvious that the RCMP deliberately refused to disclose the VICLAS information to the defense lawyer, and to the Court of Appeal of Nova Scotia. Without the proper documentation to support Glen's appeal, the Court of Appeal of Nova Scotia dismissed the case in April 2006.

It is possible that there must have been a conspiracy between the RCMP and the Nova Scotia Police, because they were doing their best to keep Glen in jail and protect Brenda's killer. Their strategy was dirty but effective. In a desperate move the prosecutor prepared a strange argument against Glen, trying to paint him as a real sexual predator capable of doing anything to get what he wanted. The prosecutor had the audacity to accuse

Glen of a 1997 rape that took place in Nova Scotia while Glen lived in British Columbia. The argument went something like this, according to published media: Since Glen's brother-in-law was working for Air Canada at the time, he had the means to fly from Vancouver to Halifax, rape the woman, and travel back to British Columbia without leaving any trace of his new crime, as his brother-in-law could get him a cheap ticket. The prosecutor did not supply any proof to support this ridiculous theory.

In Brenda's murder, the initial police investigation was overseen by a police officer named Ken, who worked at the RCMP VICLAS when the evidence collected by the other officer was destroyed. However, Innocence Canada was able to get Glen's acquittal with an extensive application, including new evidence that proved that Glen had been wrongfully convicted in 1999. As time went by, it became evident to everybody that Glen was suffering the consequences of a shameful, malicious, perverse, and disgusting police investigation, therefore in 2009, the federal government overturned the conviction, and the Justice Minister ordered a new trial. However, the Nova Scotia prosecutor decided not to re-prosecute Glen, because by then, the discredit of the whole justice system in that case was too obvious, and there would be no way of getting a conviction again.

The Federal Criminal Convictions Review Group (CCRG) investigation demonstrated that inappropriate conduct was a determinant to uphold the conviction for ten more years after the RCMP refused to provide the information collected by Constable Dave. In 2014, that group revealed that a preliminary report concluded that there was a strong possibility that Glen was the victim of a miscarriage of justice. Glen was granted bail while the review was completed, but while on bail, he was expected to always wear an electronic ankle bracelet. Glen was twenty-two years under the control and power of the justice system; seventeen years behind bars and five years with an ankle bracelet in a basement in British Columbia. He was at last free after twenty-two years under the strict control of the justice system. Shame on the whole justice system, which seems to be protecting criminals, given them full immunity and impunity.

Institutions independent of the government and the justice system were able to uncover the truth. There is no doubt that Glen's incarceration resulted from a significant conspiracy by Nova Scotia police officers.

Recent court submissions suggest that authorities colluded to destroy vital evidence, and the document points fingers at the real perpetrators of Brenda's homicide. The documents also explain why Glen was exonerated, but they were ordered to remain sealed by a court order. However, the CBC, the Canadian Press, and the Halifax Examiner successfully went to court to get the documents unsealed, while the police insisted on keeping them sealed. Once opened, the documents revealed that the RCMP had erased and destroyed all documents prepared by Constable Dave, including vital information about other potential suspects. The destruction of the files is the direct responsibility of the RCMP officers and the Halifax Regional Police. The RCMP deliberately suppressed evidence of other suspects and refused to give information to Glen and his defense lawyer.

Once the scheme was uncovered by the media, and the public became aware of it, the police used the absurd excuse of tunnel vision. However, everyone knows that this is all hogwash, and the police were fully aware of the problem they had created; it was all a coverup and lack of transparency.

I am extremely surprised at the behaviour of the police officers and the prosecutors, because in a country like this, we would assume that that kind of corruption does not happen, but it does. In every case of wrongful convictions, there seems to have been extensive dirty work done by investigators and police officers. In developing countries, that behaviour is almost normal, and the justice system is manipulated in such a way that only people with money or good connections receive justice, the rest of society is left to their own devices. It is not a secret that justice is a sort of business in many places, and most businesses are done at the highest levels of the system. This lucrative business of justice involves judges, prosecutors, defender lawyers, police officers, witnesses, and jurors.

Of the many cases of wrongful convictions presented in this book, I personally think that this one is the worst because of the many tricks and manipulation of evidence used by the police to twist the law according to their needs, including torture, threats, and extortion of their chosen victims. In addition, contempt of higher authorities, giving the impression that they are the law and can do whatever they want, knowing that they enjoy impunity and immunity. A close look at this and other cases discussed in this book shows that, unfortunately, there is no difference between the way in which the justice system functions here and the way it functions in some developing countries.

His Friend Committed the Crime but He Went to Prison Instead

Gregory, a teenage boy from St. John's Newfoundland, found his mother, Catherine dead in his bathroom with fifty-three stab wounds on her body on January 2, 1991.

When he called the police to report the crime, instead of doing their job and looking for the killer, they immediately arrested and charged him with murder, without any evidence. They made their decision based on comments that his mother, an alcoholic, had made about being afraid of her son, fearing that he could kill her one day. The police did not have witnesses, nor did they have any physical evidence, but they still decided to arrest and charge Gregory with his mother's murder, making yet another mistake that would open the door for another wrongful conviction.

In researching content for this book, I have observed that the police have the reputation of jumping to wrong conclusions, without any physical or forensic evidence; their lack of experience or incompetence pushes them to commit significant errors, which result in the wrongful conviction of people who have nothing to do with the crimes being investigated. Those police officers should be dismissed or prosecuted.

Although those investigators were sure Gregory was the killer, with time they had to accept and recognize their mistake, thanks to scientific evidence, which revealed that the young man was wrongly convicted, and the killer was instead a childhood friend named Brian. The day before Gregory discovered his mother's body, the killer had gone into Catherine's house, gaining access through a basement window. Once inside he went to her bedroom. According to him, they had been involved in a romantic relationship for some time. She had tried to end the relationship, but he wanted to keep it going. This resulted in an argument that turned violent and led him stab her repeatedly with a kitchen knife. The following day, Gregory found the body and called the police. He was arrested and charged with first degree murder but was released on bail a week later.

Gregory's trial started in September 1993, but because the prosecution did not present any evidence, the jury only listened to witnesses who spoke against Gregory, repeating the gossip that had been heard in the community about Catherine's strained relationship with her son and her concern for her safety. The jury found Gregory guilty of second-degree murder, and the judge sentenced him to life in prison without any chance for parole for fifteen years.

Gregory appealed his conviction and applied to be released on bail until his appeal would take place; he was granted bail in March 1995. His appeal started in March 1996, and the Newfoundland Court of Appeal found that the judge in charge of the trial had made many errors, so, the conviction was dismissed, and a new trial ordered. In January 1998, DNA testing proved that Gregory was not the killer, after examining the blood in a towel found at the scene of the crime and under Catherine's fingernails. Because DNA was a safe tool to confirm or dismiss a conviction, Gregory was cleared of the murder, and the judge decided not to authorize a new trial. But Gregory was not formally acquitted until November 1998. When the decision was handed down, the police had no other choice but to look for the real killer. With the results of DNA testing, it was not difficult to find the culprit. Police arrested Brian - Gregory's childhood friend, who faced with DNA evidence could not deny the killing. He confessed and explained in detail what he had done and why he had killed Catherine. It was not difficult to charge Brian because of his confession. In 2003 he pled guilty to second degree murder and was sentenced to life in prison without a chance for parole for eighteen years.

After everything was said and done, there was interest in an inquiry. As I have said before, such inquiries are only good for increasing the total cost of a wrong proceeding by the justice system, because nothing changes in the real life. There are several recommendations, but nothing ever changes. This inquiry concluded that tunnel vision and deficient police work resulted in a wrongful conviction. We have also heard from previous inquiries that this will not happen again, but it keeps happening again, and again and again.

Ismon Marroquin

I Am No Longer a Killer

Romeo was born in Ontario in 1939. In 1948, his parents sent him to a training school, where he was bullied and sexually assaulted by other children. Due to growing up in such difficult conditions, he needed survive so consequently, committed petty crimes.

In 1972, he was wrongly convicted of stabbing a firefighter named Leopold, in an apartment building in Ottawa. Mildred, Leopold's wife, gave information to the police, who drew a sketch resembling Romeo. Mildred told the police that she was not sure Romeo was the killer, so he was released. Romeo had a strong alibi anyway, because at the time of the murder, he was in Trenton, Ontario, a small town 267 kilometres from Ottawa, which meant it was impossible for him to have been the killer. However, as this story reveals, he was convicted for Leopold's murder and served thirty-one years in jail, making him the longest serving Canadian for a crime he did not commit, thanks to the incompetence and corruption of police investigating the crime, and the prosecution, who colluded with them, to charge this innocent person.

Soon after the murder, police officers went to Trenton to check Romeo's alibi and confirmed that it was true. The investigators gave the information and the documentation to the prosecutor, but they did not share that information with the defense lawyer. For unknown reasons, the documentation was lost, hidden, or misplaced during the time Romeo was in jail. Anybody would wonder if those police investigators felt remorse for the cruelty they committed, sending an innocent man to jail for thirty- one years. How do they sleep at night? Do they have families? Do they care about they own children? What type of person conceals critical information that can have major implications for the life of an innocent person? What kind of person willingly destroys the life of an innocent man and his family forever? What kind of monsters are those police officers?

The police spent four years investigating Leopold's murder, but in January 1972, Romeo was picked up by police for a robbery accusation and during the interrogation, Leopold's murder case came up. He spontaneously confessed that he was responsible for the crime. Romeo had a boyfriend named Neil, so he asked for permission to go outside to talk to him in private. When he returned, he gave a confession with details, trying to make the confession sound real. A few hours later, he recanted his confession, but nobody trusted him now because that confession was unexpected. There was much speculation about the reason for the confession. Some people though that maybe he was trying to feel important or trying to impress his boyfriend, or maybe he was just trying to play it smart because he knew he was innocent, which would be proven with his alibi. As he said later, he was just joking.

His trial started on October 16, 1972. The prosecution did not have any physical evidence, only Romeo's own confession, Leopold's wife testimony, and Neil's testimony, who testified that he had heard Romeo's confession in private. Because the defense lawyer did not know anything about Romeo's alibi, his argument was to assure the jury that Romeo was the kind of person to say false things to feel important and get attention, so he would be willing to admit to a murder he had not committed. Romeo's lawyer said that the police had lost many pieces of evidence and that his client was innocent, but the jury found him guilty, and he was sentenced to life in prison without a chance of parole for ten years. Romeo attempted to appeal his conviction to the Ontario Court of Appeal, claiming there were many problems with the police investigation, but the court dismissed his appeal. Romeo asked to have his case reopened but nothing was done; therefore, he spent the next thirty-one years in jail for a crime he did not commit.

Twenty-six years later, in 1998 his parole officer gave him some documents. He realized that in 1968, the police investigators prepared a report that stated that Romeo's alibi was true, because a Trenton service station operator confirmed to the police investigator that Romeo had been in that station between 12:00 PM and 1:00 PM the day the firefighter was killed in Ottawa. This confirmation proved that it was impossible for Romeo to have been at the scene of the murder. While police detective McCombie had ruled out Romeo as a suspect, the report was never included as part of the trial documents, which would have been the perfect evidence to prove his innocence. The report explained in detail that the investigators had been in the service station in 1968 and were convinced that Romeo told the truth about his alibi. Moreover, in the same documentation, there was the information provided to the detectives by the owner of the service station, who had told them that Romeo left his car radio in lieu of paying for a tank of gas and some small repairs. The existence of that report was never known to Romeo or his lawyer.

Romeo decided to contact Innocence Canada to ask for help. They immediately applied to determine if his conviction was a miscarriage of justice. After that he was free on bail while the Minister of Justice studied his case. On August 2, 2006, the Minister of Justice ordered the Ontario Court of Appeal to reopen Romeo's case. The main concern was why McCombie's report about Romeo's alibi had never been disclosed to the defense lawyers, which would have saved an innocent man thirty-one years of jail time. It is quite frustrating to realize the way in which police investigators and prosecutors colluded to destroy a person's entire life. The police and prosecutors must be grossly incompetent at their job, dishonest, or corrupt to lose, hide, or destroy vital documentation that can seal the fate of an innocent person. If everyone had been doing their job properly, they would have immediately shared all information with Romeo's defense, including testimonies that in any way could impact the outcome of a case.

It is unbelievable that the prosecution and police investigators, in the name of justice, would voluntarily abandon a person they know is innocent, for thirty-one years in prison. How it is possible that the whole justice system forgets about a person claiming innocence for thirty-one years without anybody listening or taking any action to correct the injustice? Is there nobody among the supervisors or other officials who cares about the travesty they are committing in the name of the law? The whole system seems to be careless and incompetent in its concern toward people who have the misfortune of passing through the doors of a detention centre.

The Court of Appeal overturned Romeo's conviction and ordered a new trial, but the prosecution did not maintain the murder charge. As a result, Romeo got his freedom on April 29, 2010, after spending thirty-one years in jail for a crime he did not commit, due to the negligence, ineptitude, and incompetence of the prosecution and the police officers who conducted the murder investigation. To add insult to the injury, the justice system denied Romeo the right to be compensated for the time he was incarcerated. However, that decision was overturned on appeal. Unfortunately, due to extensive delays in the process, Romeo did not have the chance to receive a single penny for the injustice committed against him, as he passed away on November 2, 2015, when he was still waiting to hear the court's decision about his compensation. He died in very poor conditions, being the longest-serving wrongfully convicted person in Canadian history, and the only one who never received any compensation for unjust treatment at the hands of the justice system of Canada.

Romeo's life was a real tragedy, from the beginning to the end. According to the authorities, Romeo attempted suicide several times, but was never successful. It is impossible to know how an incarcerated person might feel, especially if the person is paying for a crime they did not commit. How can someone sustain thirty-one years in jail? And how can any number of dignitaries of a government peacefully live thirty-one years knowing that they have an innocent man in jail paying for a crime he did not commit?

How can investigators, prosecutors, members of a jury, judges, lawyers, and justice ministers keep alive the torture against an innocent man for thirty-one years?

How come a legion of brilliant members of a justice system live happily in their homes, while a victim of them agonizes everyday for thirty-one years in the penitentiary until he finishes paying for a crime everybody knows he did not commit? None of them have human feelings.

Thirty-one years of suffering everyday thanks to you; and you, and you. Do not you feel remorse for your cruelty?

We will have real justice only when these white collar criminals pay for their crimes, because accusing a person of a crime he did not commit is a CRIME and those responsible must be prosecuted. The criminals are wrongfully convicting innocent people. Enough!!!

After Twenty-Three Years in Prison, His Conviction Was Overturned

Frank was a German programmer, and after spending some time in the army, he became unemployed for three years. He then took on a job as a hair stylist and later started selling small quantities of drugs to some customers. He got to meet some important people in the drug business. In 1986, a well-known drug dealer was killed; to solve the case, the police and the prosecutor made a deal with another drug dealer to testify against Frank, so that he could be charged with the crime. At that time, the chief prosecutor was an infamous lawyer, known for purposely getting convictions on innocent people for reasons that nobody knew or understood. His behaviour was criticized by every honest lawyer working in the field, but unfortunately, nobody had the courage to file a complaint against him or denounce his dishonesty and unprofessional behaviour. It was common knowledge that he would look for false evidence or false witnesses to win a case, without caring about the consequences.

Frank had the misfortune of being arrested and accused of killing the drug dealer. Once Frank was chosen, the chief prosecutor and the police investigators, built a case against him. He ended up being wrongfully convicted of first-degree murder in 1987 and sentenced to life in prison; a crime that Frank steadily denied from the day of his arrest. Unfortunately, his fate had been sealed by the police and the prosecutor. Even though Frank did not pull the trigger, he was accused of ordering the murder. This accusation was based on false testimony provided by his partner in exchange for exoneration of his own crime of drug trafficking and distribution. While Frank did not have anything to do with the drug dealer's murder, he was framed by the complicity of the chief prosecutor and the police, who decided to hide the evidence that proved the killer was somebody else. Frank's partner was the only person who knew where Frank hid drugs and money inside his home. When the police went to his home, armed with a search warrant, they did not waste any time; they went directly to the place where the money and drugs were hidden.

Years later it became known that his partner knew who the real killer was and had provided that information to the police in a statement the day before Frank was arrested; therefore, it was easy to charge him with a murder he did not commit, as the prosecution, police, and special witness had decided to frame him. This type of behaviour can be expected from a drug dealer, but not from the authorities in charge of applying the law. The people who framed Frank kept silent about the statement Frank's partner gave to police, where he assured them that Frank was not the killer.

However, it was already decided that Frank would go to jail. That complicity was a real crime, because all of them knew that the man they were sending to jail was innocent.

In the various stories presented in this book, it is interesting to see how police investigators and prosecutors engage in the same unethical behaviour repeatedly with absolute impunity. And to make things worse, the crimes they commit are in the name of the law they are supposed to uphold. They use the law as a shield to avoid prosecution, but they know that they are the real criminals.

Years later everybody was sure that Frank would have never been convicted if in 1987 that crucial evidence had been shared with the defense lawyer during the trial. That aberration of justice cost Frank twenty-three years in jail before being freed on bail in 2009.

Innocence Canada submitted a ministerial review application on Frank's behalf to the Minister of Justice in 2014, who decided that maybe Frank's case was a miscarriage of justice and ordered the Manitoba Court of Appeal to conduct a review. In November 2018, the Manitoba Court of Appeal annulled Frank's murder conviction, and at the same time, the court decided that it would be unfair to order a second trial after thirty years, therefore the court entered a judicial stay of proceedings. Judges of the Court of Appeal ruled that Frank was denied vital information that would have helped his lawyer with his defense when he was convicted of first-degree murder in 1987. Later it became known that the same key witness had given a statement to the police, informing them that the shooter was somebody else. The police had received the information in writing, had kept it, and in complicity with the prosecutor, decided not to share it with the defense.

Frank was forced to spend the best years of his life behind bars because of the barbaric actions of a group of wicked government employees. Those heading up the provincial justice system should be ashamed of what the system represents for people like Frank; a system that can violate the rights of individuals, abuse power, and act with little or no regard for the dignity of those accused of crimes, specially when they know that those accused are innocent people. The inherent complicity of these people at the top of the justice system is unacceptable in a country where the law is supposed to protect those who abide by it and to respect the rights of all. In Frank's case the farse was not an accident; everything was planned with malice, bad intention, and the willingness to do enough damage for incontestable reasons. And while there is more back and forth about paying compensation for the damage caused, everything converges at a point where the applicant was wrongfully convicted, due to a carefully crafted plan. If this is true, the government should stop the farse and pay any compensation sooner, rather than later.

Conviction Overturned Using DNA

Kyle, a nineteen-year-old, young man, attended a rock concert in June 1990 at a ski resort close to the community of Roseisle in Manitoba. Many people attended the event, including his classmate Brigitte, a sixteen-year-old high school student and Timothy, a seventeen-year-old boy. All three attended separately. There was drinking, dancing, and drugs at the event. At about 1:30 AM, Timothy and Brigitte were dancing together and fondling each other. After a while, they went to a secluded and wooded area. At about the same time, Kyle went to the washroom. When he returned, he told his friend John that he had seen Brigitte with a guy going to the wooded place. When Timothy returned to the party, between 4:00 and 4:30 AM from the wooded area, Brigitte was no longer with him. His face and clothes were covered in mud, and he had scratches on his face and hands. Moreover, he had blood on his chin. His appearance gave the impression that he had been in a big fight. He explained that an unknown guy attacked him and knocked him out.

Kyle and John separated between 2:00 and 2:30 AM. Kyle left the music festival between 4:30 and 5:00 AM by car, and according to everybody who saw him leave, he was clean and without any marks on his clothes, face, arms, or other visible parts of his body. According to people at the party, when Timothy left the dance area, he and a friend had gone to set fire to some stuff that was in a barrel close to the entrance of the festival area. Early the next morning, Brigitte's naked body was discovered in the wooded area lying in a creek; she had been killed sadistically, something only a sexual psychopath could do. She had been struck on different parts of her body with a heavy object and then strangled.[1]

The investigators interviewed many people who had attended the festival, including Timothy and Kyle. The RCMP visited Timothy at his home two days after the murder and noted visible marks on his face and hands, however, the police did not take a statement from him at that time because he was underage, and his parents were not present. When the police were able to take a statement from Timothy, he admitted, without any hesitation to having had consensual sex with Brigitte, but he said that after that, he was attacked by an unknown person, who knocked him unconscious. Police asked him for a description of his attacker, and he said something that made the police jump to the conclusion that the attacker was Kyle. In a second statement, Timothy pointed to Kyle as his attacker and accused Kyle of killing Brigitte. He claimed that while Kyle was brutally attacking the defenseless girl, he told Timothy to punch Brigitte's face, which he did out of fear for his own safety.

The problem was that everybody who had been at the party had confirmed that they had not seen anything wrong with Kyle's body or clothes throughout the night. He had been at the concert the whole time and had left in a car. The same people had also indicated that Timothy looked different after returning from the wooded area, and that he had mud all over his face and clothing, plus blood on his chin, hands, and shoes. It was clear that the murder of the young girl was the work of a psychopath or sadist who enjoyed the pain of his victim. It seemed that killing her was not enough; he also introduced a sharp, long object into her vagina and anus, and after that he took pleasure in strangling her. Both Timothy and Kyle were charged with first degree murder.

At Timothy's trial, the prosecution provided forensic evidence. They presented blood from Brigitte on Timothy's shoes, Timothy's pubic hair on her sock, and another on her pants. Implicating Kyle in the crime was a single hair found on Brigitte sweatshirt, which was consistent with a hair he had provided voluntarily to police investigators. While Timothy's case was sent to adult court, the Crown had doubts about Kyle's involvement in the crime, but the RCMP insisted that Kyle was a killer and started looking for ways to convict him. In December 1990, Kyle's preliminary hearing got a stay of proceedings.

After that decision and because the RCMP had only a hair incriminating Kyle, they started looking for jailhouse informants to build a strong case against the accused. The RCMP interviewed over twenty inmates, trying to find people willing to testify that they had heard Kyle confess to the murder. Five inmates were willing to testify against Kyle, but in the end, the prosecution accepted only one who seemed to be credible. His name was Jeffery. During the trial, the defense proved that the witness was lying, which Jeffery admitted, but inexplicably, the prosecution did not accept that he was lying and continued with the case, determined to implicate Kyle in the crime.

The RCMP had decided to get a confession from Kyle, so, they put into action a Canadian interrogation technique called "Mr. Big Operation", which essentially consists of creating a fictional crime organization to gain the trust of the targeted person and motivate him to join, but first, he must prove that he's a criminal like the other members. The RCMP designated four police officers with the mission to include Kyle as a prospect to get easy money through the crime. At the beginning he was reluctant, however, in the end, he decided to lie so he could be accepted into the organization.

He told the guys that he had killed Brigitte, a confession they were waiting to hear, to arrest and charge him for the murder of the girl. Kyle was re-arrested on June 25, 1991, for Brigitte's murder. On February 28, 1992, Kyle and Timothy were convicted of first-degree murder. Both appealed the conviction, but on July 7, 1993, the Manitoba Court of Appeal upheld Kyle's conviction and ordered a new trial for Timothy, who committed suicide before being retried. On December 2, 1993, the Supreme Court of Canada confirmed the decision of the Manitoba Court of Appeal about upholding Kyle's conviction.

In 2004 a Forensic Review Committee took the hair used to convict Kyle and sent it to be examined by a laboratory using DNA, which was at the time, a new, infallible tool. The DNA proved that the hair did not belong to Kyle. That hair had been the only evidence the prosecution had against the accused man; however, nobody in the justice system moved a finger to release Kyle from jail.

On September 13, 2004, Innocence Canada applied on Kyle's behalf to the Minister of Justice, for ministerial review of his conviction. On November 4, 2005, Kyle was granted bail, more than thirteen years after he was convicted for a crime he did not commit. The federal minister ordered a new trial and four years later Kyle was cleared of Brigitte's murder. On October 23, 2009, the Manitoba Deputy Attorney General asked that he be officially acquitted, with no compensation and no public inquiry into his wrongful conviction. Kyle spent fourteen years in jail and nineteen under the control of the justice system for a crime he did not commit.

You do not have to be a lawyer to understand that in Kyle's case, justice was not served. The Justice system insisted on having an innocent man under its control for no reason since the DNA test had already proven, in 2004, that he was innocent of the crime, and it was then that he should have been freed with compensation and a formal apology. Instead, he remained guilty until 2009, when he was acquitted. To add insult to injury, the RCMP and the Attorney General's office refused to take responsibility for his wrongful conviction, maintaining that the damage he had suffered was of his own doing for not denouncing or destroying the traps thrown at him by the RCMP. Shame on all those involved with this injustice. By imposing their arbitrary decisions, they show that they are the law or that they are above the law. They do not have any respect for human beings.

Clearly speaking, any wrongdoing in cases like Kyle's is completely the government's responsibility. It is ludicrous to think that the government, through the justice system, will spend hundreds of thousands of dollars fabricating cases against innocent people; coercing, instructing, and preparing criminals to testify against somebody who is defending his reputation or freedom. And after all this money is wasted, and the life of an innocent person is ruined; the justice system refuses to pay compensation. In a democratic society, to arrest and charge an innocent person, and violate his civil rights in the name of the law, looks very much like a kidnapping in countries without freedom. Somebody should be accountable for taking away a person's freedom for fourteen years, or for any amount of that, for that matter. Not taking responsibility for that, should be a crime, and all those responsible should pay the price.

Hiding relevant evidence from the defense, helped to convict Kyle, because he did not know why he was a suspect. Knowing the way police officers have worked in previous similar cases, it is no surprise to learn that the officers in charge of the investigation influenced Timothy to blame Kyle for the crime, a person without any forensic evidence against him. It was later discovered that the RCMP knew that Timothy was a satanist, but they did not share that information with the defense; it was also known that when Timothy was fourteen years old, he had forced his way into the house of a neighbour girl and pulled down her underwear; however, that information was kept from the defense. Timothy also stated at some point that maybe Kyle was not the killer, but that information was not provided to the defense either. This all points to the fact that police investigators did not conduct a fair investigation but were interested in implicating Kyle in the crime.

There are criminal cases in which the investigators consider that the public is foolish and will accept anything without any doubt; this is one of those cases. The media presented all the evidence, while the prosecution adjusted the evidence to their own interests or decisions. This is another example of forensic evidence that was collected but not shared with the defense. The victim had teeth marks on her breasts and arm; Kyle voluntarily provided a sample that did not match the marks on the victim's body, but the prosecution decided to stay the charge against him even though Timothy, the person with a lot of forensic information on his face, arms, shoes, and clothes, refused to provide any sample.

Kyle got bail, his freedom, and eventually his acquittal, but he will forever keep the stigma of being a convicted killer, thanks to the deficient and dirty work of the police and corrupt prosecution.

Is Manitoba the Wrongful Conviction Capital of Canada?

There are people, especially politicians, academics, and justice system officials who are always trying to defend the undefendable, looking for excuses to justify the errors or mistakes made during the process of wrongful convictions. They avoid accepting the facts or real causes of these convictions. These people do not like to call things by their real name: incompetence, dishonesty, corruption, or abuse of power. There was a time when an insensible, corrupt, and dishonest prosecutor would send innocent people to jail, and once there, their lives became a nightmare. He knew exactly what he was doing and apparently, he enjoyed destroying the lives of his selected victims. Once in jail, a sinister chain of events would unfold against the wrongfully convicted, including the use of false documentation, false statements, fabricated witnesses, and more, to ensure the wrongfully convicted would remain in jail for an indeterminate period of time. This prosecutor would not share or disclose any evidence to the defense team, making everything more difficult for the wrongfully convicted. While most people already knew about this unethical behaviour, they never said anything due to complicity, fear, or convenience. Whatever the case, the results of this despicable behaviour were obvious to all. The failure of the entire justice system would start in the prosecutor's office, who did not do his job ethically much of the time, although nobody knows why. He was a prosecutor everybody tried to avoid, given his reputation. This man inflicted too much damage on the judicial system, and it seemed that everybody was afraid of him, but nobody would speak up.

He played a lead role in every case resulting in a wrongful conviction, and he did not care and neither did others within the system as he engaged in the same behaviour over, and over again. The man seemed to be untouchable, and never changed his behaviour until retirement. The basis for his malefic attitude was a mystery, and nobody was able to uncover his powerful connections. After he retired the entire system changed for the better, and the wrongful convictions were not as common. Whoever wants to review his conduct as a prosecutor, will find that most of his work was dishonest and corrupt. It is difficult to understand why his superiors did not replace him to stop the damage he was inflicting on the entire justice system. Every one of his wrongful convictions put a dent in the credibility of the provincial justice system, which led people to start thinking that this province was the wrongful conviction capital of the country. Removing or changing that bad reputation, surely will take many years.

If DNA has been available as an indisputable mechanism to prove evidence for more than three decades, then why were there so many wrongful convictions after 1990? This shows that in some places it does not matter what kind of scientific tools are available to prove innocence or culpability. Even with the best available resources, our prosecutors look for a way to get a conviction, because it is good for their personal ambition and reputation.

When a wrongful conviction occurs with the knowledge and mutism of lawyers, prosecutors, witnesses, and investigators, without a positive complaint, it means that something is wrong and easily the whole system could get rotten. When that kind of distortion of justice applies, the public becomes suspicious and soon realizes that the courts are not applying the laws properly. Instead, it is a kind of business where the principal actors are pocketing big amounts of money, so, corruption must be kept alive for the business to thrive.

If the scientific tools are available, they should be used right at the start of any investigation to avoid major blunders that can have dire consequences; once a mistake is made it is difficult to go back and fix the problem. The first interrogation should be used to determine if the suspicious person is the only suspect or whether there are others, and before arresting and charging anybody, detectives must be very clear about different possibilities and never make an arrest in a rush. They should never send somebody to jail without being absolutely convinced that the right person is being charged.

The detectives are the face of the justice system, if they do a bad job, the whole process may be impacted, therefore those detectives must work professionally to gain the confidence of the system, ensuring justice is administered with transparency and accountability. One excuse for errors or misconduct that has been used repeatedly in wrongful convictions is tunnel vision; that excuse would be avoided for ever if every step of the investigation is done in an honest and professional way. If the bad tactics persist, it would mean that the system is already rotten, and the corruption will be difficult to eradicate from the justice system.

The most common injustice cited by defense lawyers includes unprepared lawyers, inappropriate witnesses, failure to get evidence from the prosecution, perjured testimonies, bad faith against the suspect, contaminated evidence, information obtained from prison inmates, tunnel vision, fabrication, changing, or destroying evidence by police investigators.

In Canada, demonstrating that a person has been wrongfully convicted, sometimes can take longer that the time they must spend in jail for the crime. It is more convenient to do time in jail for any conviction, than trying to convince the authorities that they are wrong about the conviction. The time that a person will spend behind bars if they take the chance and accept culpability may sometimes be less than if they claim his rights in the application of the law. It seems that in the justice system nobody takes their responsibilities seriously because everybody works in slow motion without caring about the person who is in jail waiting a decision depending on the public servants of the justice system. That behaviour must change as soon as possible, otherwise, the new technology will result useless.

Somebody must have the courage to remove all existing red tape in the justice system. The red tape that makes these types of cases move in slow motion. Shame on every official ignoring the fate of those wrongfully convicted human beings who are behind bars, hoping that someday, somebody will look at their case and act.

HUNTING SEASON

Always Eager to Pull the Trigger

John Joseph, a thirty-six-year-old Indigenous leader from Wasagamack First Nation, who lived in Winnipeg, one night decided to go out with friends on March 8, 1988, like he had done many times before. He never thought that this would be the last time. They parted ways past mid night and instead of taking a taxi, he decided to walk along Logan Avenue. Nothing would have happened if he had not had the misfortune of encountering a police officer on his way home. While John Joseph was having fun with his friends, a car had been stolen by two young boys in another part of the city. Those boys would later be identified as Pruden and Allan.

When the police were informed of the stolen car, a search started in the vicinity of the area where John Joseph was drinking with friends. At about 2:00 AM, when the friends parted ways, police units were informed that the boys who had stolen the vehicle had been arrested and were in police custody. All officers were working in pairs; however, the officer who killed John Joseph was walking alone, back to where his partner was waiting for him in the police cruiser with Allan, one of the boys who had stolen the vehicle.

Nobody knows exactly what happened during the encounter with Joseph, but somehow this police officer said (since John Joseph could not give his own version of events, for obvious reasons) that John Joseph had been shot during a scuffle with him. However, Allan later testified that when the officer met his partner back in the cruiser, he had told her that it happened so fast when he pulled the trigger. There were no witnesses, so, the officer explained his actions to the officers, but each time, he gave a different version about the events. According to him, when he saw a man walking on the street, he asked him for identification. There was no reason for this, since he already knew that the robbers were already in custody. He said that the man refused to give an identification to him, so, he grabbed the man and a scuffle unfolded; suddenly, his pistol activated itself, putting a bullet in the middle of Joseph's chest, who minutes earlier was minding his own business, going home and unarmed.

There were a lot of discrepancies in the testimonies of the officer who participated in the chain of events the night of the shooting, which were confirmed by Pruden, the other car thief, who gave a different version from those given by the officers. A cover up started taking place immediately, where the main purpose was to blame the innocent man for his own death; his crime had been to cross paths with a police officer that fateful night.

The public knows that when the police investigate themselves it is not difficult to exonerate their members of any wrongdoing, but only themselves will trust in the result of the investigation. This was an even easier case, because there were no impartial witnesses; there were only two actors and one of them was dead. That murder was solved by police in record time, because the day after the shooting, the department's Firearms Board of Enquiry, sent its report to the Police Chief, clearing the police officer of any wrongdoing. The report read as though every member of the board was an eyewitness to the shooting. The afternoon of the same day, the Chief gave a report to the news media, indicating that the officer had been cleared of any wrongdoing because the dead person had assaulted the officer. This statement was concerning as it left no doubt that the dead man had assaulted the police officer. After an inquest the judge in charge exonerated the police officer of any wrongdoing. It seemed like everyone was following a principle written in a book that every member of the organization must know by heart. Nothing different and nothing unexpected. Only the public were scratching their heads. And maybe the police officer who shot and killed the Indigenous man was surprised at the way his colleagues and the system ensured that all the facts fit together to exonerate him.

From that day on, a major problem started to unfold between Indigenous people and the police department. People were asking for justice, and the police justified the killing of the unarmed man, who had presumably assaulted and overpowered an armed police officer. People followed the case with special interest and incredulity. With time things became worse, particularly when the police decided to investigate the lawyer representing Joseph's family in the case against the officer who had killed Joseph. This was a prominent lawyer in the city, who was now being accused of sexual assault.

This situation made the public think that the accusation was revenge for his work in the case. A scary controversy for regular citizens since nobody can claim anything about police behaviour without running the risk of reprisals. It was known that a city commissioner recommended a reorganization of the police crime department because some of its members disliked lawyers, journalists, and politicians. If lawyers, journalists, and politicians fear the police, what can be said about regular citizens?

Two councillors reported that they had had some problems with the police, and now they felt harassed. One of the councillors explained that somebody close to the police department told him that police cruisers were carrying his licence plate number on their dashboard. Also, sometimes they tried to intimidate him by parking their cruisers in front of or close to his home. The other councillor said that he had been harassed by police pulling him over many times, they gave him traffic tickets. The harassment had been so frequent that in eight days he got ten tickets.

According to the recommendation of the commissioner, four police officers were transferred from the crime unit to another unit, but they disagreed with the order and made a legal complaint, forcing the respective authorities to make a deal with them. This deal resulted in better positions, credits, and benefits for the police officers. As a result, one officer retired with benefits, another went back to the crime division, and the other two received four weeks of holidays within the next twenty-four months, but everything was okay because the taxpayers absorbed everything, and the public is the loser. All this mess seemed to be related to the way the police investigated, arrested, and charged John Joseph's lawyer. At the end of the controversy, an inquiry exonerated the police officer and made recommendations that nobody will remember in a short time.

Ismon Marroquin

After Killing a Man Police Refuse a Breathalyzer

Abraham had been accused of selling small quantities of illegal drugs in a north end Winnipeg neighbourhood, and on December 16, 1997, he paid with his life for this alleged crime. On that day a group of police officers had attended a Christmas party where alcohol had been served. After the party, some of them decided to execute a search warrant at 479 Dufferin Avenue to look for Abraham. Back at police headquarters, before attending the Christmas party eight of them had prepared to participate in the mission and according to the information they later provided it appeared that this preparation was enough for a battlefield. Although only one man was the target of the operation, a crew of eight officers went with a large ram made of solid steel and weighing between eighty and one hundred pounds. It needed to be operated by to men to take down the door of the house. They also had pry bars, pepper spray, hasps, a tool similar to a baton but much more effective; because it is used to put someone down to facilitate his arrest, raid jackets with the police logo, handcuffs, and firearms.

Armed with a search warrant, the eight police officers, who had just left the party where alcohol had been served, went to Abraham's home after 10:00 PM looking for him; four of them went to the back of the house, and four went to the front. Abraham, a long-distance truck driver, was at home with his wife and his dog, enjoying a nice time on a peaceful night. According to the information given later by the officers, they knocked on the door, but nobody answered, so, they proceeded to break the rear door with the ram to enter the house. But when the officers were trying to break the door, Abraham came and hit an officer on the leg with a bat, which gave the uniformed man the authority to discharge his weapon and kill Abraham.

Common sense tells us that whenever somebody is trying to break into our home and endanger our family, it is our duty to defend our family and our property, which is what Abraham was trying to do when he was killed. It was known that he was blind in one eye, had cancer, and was a convicted small drug trafficker. If the police officers had all the advantages on their side, such as an elaborate plan, the surprise element, the time chosen by them, the complicity of the night, the power of the uniforms, the weapons, and the advantage of the number of officers, they did not have to kill the man. This killing only proves lack of preparation, lack of professionalism, bad intentions, or the will to hurt or kill someone. Without the intention of killing, eight men, would surely have the necessary skills to subdue a man who is sick and blind in an eye.

The problem is that many officers feel compelled to use the revolver. After all, they know, that no matter what happens, they will be exonerated by the system, as was the result of this investigation. Why did they choose to execute the search warrant close to midnight and after having attended the party and being under the influence of alcohol. Even in developing countries, any search warrant must be enforced from 6:00 AM to 6:00 PM, and never during night hours, when it is highly likely to find a family with children at the residence. People inside the house have the right to defend their family and property from any attack, which is considered a basic and fundamental right of every person in the world, however in some parts of Canada, this can be problematic. For example, in British Columbia, an old man who tried to defend himself and his home from an intruder, was charged with aggravated assault.

It is concerning that police sometimes fire to kill when they are called to a home or go to execute a search warrant, whenever people call the police, it is because they need help, not to aggravate their situation. When police are dispatched to a home, they should go thinking that their responsibility is to help those in need; therefore, they should be very careful when talking to people and never make any threats or assumptions. Police officers must act with calm, use the best words they can, and never use their weapons to de-escalate a tense situation; their chosen words should be enough to solve the problem. If there is a domestic altercation, police should be able to make peace, instead of taking a person to jail or, worse, injuring or killing a member of the family. If police use their weapons, it is to kill, because if they do not intend to kill, they would try to find other ways to subdue the person.

According to news stories associated with Abraham's killing, the officers who executed the search warrant were impaired by alcohol, yet they still went to Abraham house to enforce a search warrant against him. They could have waited until the next day, but they chose to go intoxicated instead. Seven of the officers refused to give blood samples to determine if they were intoxicated at the time of the killing. If we applied the same rules to the police as citizens face when asked to take a breathalyzer test or give a blood sample, the seven officers who refused to give a blood sample would automatically be considered guilty.

The behaviour of these officers is not strange, since their defense lawyer, who was the counsel for the Police Association, expressed disdain for the blood sample requirement, saying with an absolute lack of respect for the dead man and his family that a big issue had been made out of nothing. Of course, he has de right to give an opinion about the case to justify his clients, but he can not say that they are innocent if he does not have the whole picture about what happened before and during the killing. He was not a witness to the incident. Whatever the case, the counsel did not have to worry about the consequences of the investigation because the officers were being investigated by their own, in violation of one of the most important recommendations during the Aboriginal Justice Inquiry.

Whenever there is an internal investigation, it is highly possible that there will be a cover up. People have the right to think that something is wrong, because in the past, the police have given enough reason for people to think that way. During the investigation of this murder, something was not right. It was similar to the killing of John Joseph, where the police force rushed to clear the officer without any investigation. It is almost guaranteed that if these investigations were done by external and impartial investigators, many police officers would be serving long jail sentences. The behaviour of many police officers is known to the public, and it is known that the police lie to protect each other, even in an era where social media can show clear proof of their wrongdoings, like in the cases of Rodney King, George Floyd, and Robert Dziekanski. An internal police investigation recommended that the police officers who killed Abraham not be charged for the crime, because, according to the investigation, there were no grounds to lay charges.

Man Killed by Police in Front of Many Witnesses.

Mark Norman was killed by three Simcoe Police officers in the parking lot of Tim Hortons on Barrie Street on Bradford Ontario; he was running for his life in front of police officers (two men and one woman), who had been looking for him the whole night, according to their statement. Police considered the man armed and dangerous, because the day before, a man was shot outside a tavern in downtown Bradford, two blocks away from Tim Hortons. The police identified the man as Mark Norman because of the special tattoos the shooter had on his body. A search was immediately initiated by police, accompanied by tracker dogs.

It is regrettable that the police do not look for ways to arrest a suspect without a fatal epilogue because in this case, as soon as the officer saw the suspect, they drew their weapons and started running behind the scared man. There have been many cases when the police have used their pistols and killed suspects, which may be why some suspected criminals try to avoid them instead of surrendering. When the police officers got close to Mark in the parking lot, they asked him to stop, but he did not. Maybe he knew they would kill him, so he kept walking and said, I will be back, guys.

There were lot of customers around, but the three police officers did not seem to care about the safety of innocent people. All three fired into the back of the man and killed him; afterwards, they turned over the corpse, hand cuffed him, and charged him, a ridiculous and shameful action by the officers. Many witnesses could not believe what they were seeing. A group of police officers killing an unarmed man and hand cuffing his corpse. Shame on those officers.

A few minutes later, two paramedics showed up and started giving cardiopulmonary resuscitation to the cadaver, but soon they realized he was already dead. One witness saw the police officers with their weapons drawn while they were running behind the man, and no one saw a gun in possession of the dead man. It would be interesting to read the report from each of those officers. It was concerning to everybody at the scene that the officers killed the man in front of many onlookers, a situation many considered dangerous and showing a lack of respect for the witnesses of the killing. Behind the police officers a group of teenagers were shouting abuse; and were encouraging Mark not to do what the police were asking; they were telling him that the police could not shoot him because that is the law in Canada. Those inexperienced teenagers do not know that the law is one thing, and what police do on the streets is something very different. And apparently, what they do is done with absolute impunity as there are no consequences for those kinds of crimes committed by these public servants enforcing the laws. Those shocking spectacles are seen frequently by many people around the country, and they are executed by official shooters.

All the witnesses agreed that the police officers were pointing at his back the whole time and were telling him to stop, but nobody gave him a warning and suddenly the three officers just pulled the trigger using his back as a common target. It was a premeditated crime, and surely, if they had not killed him, their adrenaline would have been running high for a long time. Shame on those people, owners of the law.

RCMP Officers Killed an Innocent Newcomer at Vancouver Airport

Robert, a forty-year-old man from Poland, left his native country on October 13, 2007, to reunite in Canada with his mother Zofia, who had been living in Vancouver, since 1999. Zofia was a single mother, and Robert was her only child. They decided that Robert would immigrate to Canada to be together again in this peaceful and safe country. Unfortunately, they did not consider the many difficulties that Robert would face on his arrival at this new country, because he could not speak English. After a very long trip traveling from Poland, Robert arrived in his new country and immediately began the immigration process while his mother waited outside.

Three hours after his expected arrival, Zofia asked several staff, in her best English, about Robert, but nobody could help her. Based on my own experience, I wonder if maybe nobody was willing to help her, given the way in which she spoke English. She thought that maybe Robert had missed a flight and had not arrived that day, at which point, she decided to go home. Later that day, in the early hours of October 14, 2007, Robert /

lost his life inside the airport at the hands of RCMP officers who did not have enough patience, competence, and professionalism to determine why a person with an evident lack of English was inside a prohibited area of the airport. Being able to speak English was the first thing he needed to explain why he was where he was, but the airport failed to look for a translator. It is unbelievable that even security guards had not bothered to ask him why he was in that area for such a long time.

During the attack on Robert by four RCMP officers, one security guard looked at them and supervised the whole process of Robert's murder. Minutes before, the same guard was seen in the video with other staff, passively looking at Robert and what he was doing before he was tasered. That security staffer seems to be the one who called the RCMP officers, who arrived quickly. It was clear that they did not lose time trying to help the language handicapped man; instead, they proceeded to taser him and finish him off. From that moment on, a series of lies, perjuries and controversies took place to justify the attitude of the Mounties. They displayed a defensive attitude to justify their violent action, until a video appeared. The whole system failed Robert. When he arrived and approached the immigration office to check his passport, the staff asked Robert the routine questions, but realized that he did not speak the language and needed help. If the airport had the resources, it was just a matter of making an internal telephone call and asking for somebody to come and help the man; but if the airport did not have that kind of service, it was truly lacking something that should be available in this country. But in either case, it should not have let a newly arrived person walk around without any help. Every worker who saw Robert during the nine hours he was wandering inside the airport, without asking him who he was or what he was doing in a restricted area, must be ashamed and somehow responsible for his death. Any human being with a little concern, would avoid the tragedy faced by an innocent and peaceful immigrant, who lost all his dreams inside the Vancouver airport that terrible night.

According to Zofia, she arrived on time at the airport, but she made the mistake of waiting for him in a different place while he was still inside waiting for her in a secluded area, without knowing she would not be able to access that space. In the confusion, Robert waited for his mother inside the airport for ten hours. During that time, he did not eat or speak with anybody; he got frustrated, impatient and maybe angry because he did not know what to do after waiting ten hours in a strange place. By then, his mother had left, thinking that her son had not arrived.

With increasing frustration from the extremely long trip, lack of sleep, lack of food, the ten-hour wait and not understanding the language, Robert eventually threw some furniture to get the attention of the people who were in front of him. When the security guards realized what Robert was doing, instead of assisting him, they called the police to control the situation. Unfortunately, it does not seem that the police have a good handle on human relations, or maybe it is not part of their training. Instead of looking for a human, normal, simple, and peaceful solution, they solved the problem by tasering Robert, attacking him until he died.

The four RCMP police officers who arrived where Robert had spent hours waiting for his mother immediately tasered him. They knelt over him, and handcuffed him face down, without any intent of looking for other means to deal with him or communicate with him. They did not bother to investigate why he was there and what was going on, and without any warning, the four police officers jumped over the fence Robert had used to barricade himself and started tasering, pinning him down, and handcuffing him until he was dead. This all took about two minutes. As Robert was a normal person coming from another country for the very first time in his life, can we guess as his last thoughts about the way he was treated by the men wearing the uniform that make people proud of this country? Maybe when he saw those guys, empowered by the uniform, coming toward him, he thought they were going to help him. Wrong. They were going to end his life. Before he died, one of the officers pressed him to the floor with one of his knees, like the way George Floyd was killed in the U.S by a police officer who was later convicted and sentenced to over twenty years behind bars for the crime. But in Canada, the uniformed men who killed Robert are free, except for one, who was sentenced to thirty months behind bars; but not for the murder, but for the perjury after a long legal battle in which Robert's mother was the only one fighting against the whole legal system until the killing was forgotten. Zofia went back to her country to mourn the murder of her only son. She died of a stroke in Poland on November 18, 2019.

One traveller who witnessed Robert's killing was able to record everything while waiting for his luggage at the baggage carousel, but after the police killed Robert, the officers confiscated his camera. When the man recovered it, there was no evidence of the murder, as the police had altered the memory card. The police officers involved in the killing presented their superiors with a common version of events for many of these types of crimes, where they accuse the dead of belligerence, assaulting a police officer, or resisting arrest. The officers reported that Robert attacked them, and that was why they used lethal force. However, the truth later came to light when the video taken by the young man was released. At this point, the four RCMP officers changed their version, yet insisted they were innocent, despite the evidence the public had already seen.

Robert's death was regrettable because he was never a threat to the RCMP officers who killed him. It was obvious to everybody who saw the video that the man was killed without any opportunity to say why he was in that place, or why he was in this country, without speaking the language of his killers, who were supposed to protect him. In August 2007 (two months before this event), the RCMP had changed their protocols, suggesting that multiple taser shocks may be appropriate under certain circumstances. It is possible that Robert was the first victim of these new RCMP protocols. On December 12, 2008, the Criminal Justice Branch of British Columbia determined that the force these officers used was necessary and reasonable, so criminal charges were not pressed. They remained on duty, and the supervisor resigned from the force on July 20, 2012, according to news reports.

The Braidwood Inquiry recommended a revision of the decision of December 2008. As a result, all four officers were charged with perjury. On June 22, 2015, Constable Millington was sentenced to thirty months and Constable Robinson to two years for perjury. The spokesman committed suicide in 2013 when it was discovered that he had been lying about Robert's murder on behalf of the institution. After his death, his wife said that he was made a pariah and demoted by the RCMP and that he was prevented from correcting his public statements after he found out the truth. This uniformed man proved that he had dignity, and he preferred to be dead than face the ridicule of society, who already knew that the officers were lying and using him as a scapegoat.

Robert's murder was not a mistake because the officers had the time and the opportunity to show the world that whoever comes to this country will be protected by the same laws that apply to their own citizens. In the video the public was able to see the way in which a new immigrant was treated by four of their honourable members of the RCMP, and during the long discourse that took place about the murder, the public also learned that seventeen other people had also been killed by police with the use of taser guns, which is an extremely high number for continuing use of such lethal weapon. To everyone's surprise, both the police and the manufacturer of taser guns had the audacity to say that such deaths are the result of pre-existing medical conditions and not the electrical shocks.

Man Trapped Like a Rabbit

Mark was killed by police officers on November 6, 2015, at the corner of Kenaston Boulevard and Grant Avenue after a chase by almost forty police officers with over thirty police cruisers. With all those resources assigned to a single chase, one would expect that the suspect would be apprehended alive, and not killed. Further, the number of resources committed to one suspect would indicate that the person was heavily armed and dangerous. Mark was not armed when he was killed by police. The resulting investigation concluded that the murder was justified, which was an expected outcome, given the long history of similar investigations. However, as time progressed, it was a surprise to learn that the police officers who shot Mark were charged with murder.

After the killing, the public learned that police knew that Mark was suicidal, but instead of looking for professional help for him, they decided it was better to end his life with a rain of bullets. Other reasons to justify the murder were that he was suffering depression, had a lot of debt, had been laid off from his work in Alberta, had lost his driver's licence, was in a bad relationship with his girlfriend; and for all of that, he wanted to die. Everything started when a police officer saw him driving erratically on the streets; she reported the case, and in a matter of minutes more than thirty police cars were participating in the chase. When the police corralled Mark, instead of looking for ways to arrest him, they started looking for the best spot to shoot him. When Mark realized that his fate was to face an imminent death, he stoically faced the firing squad preparing to kill him. When they started firing, it seemed like they were having fun while discharging their guns with a rain of bullets impacting on their target. When everything was over, some police officers were taking pride in the way they were able to kill a defenseless and distraught man.

During the inquest the public learned a very important secret of police training through a statement made by one of the shooters, Constable Ragetli, who said that police is trained to keep shooting until the target is dead, which must be understood as there is no mercy at all, once the shooters start firing. That explains why some officers are so eager to pull the trigger. In many simple cases that would warrant simple solutions people die in encounters with the police. An expert in the use of force explained that police officers are not required to wait for a gun to be pointed at them. It is terrifying to know that police can start firing as soon as they feel compelled to do it. In media reports, a police training expert indicated that one of the police training methods is the Rambo style training, in which an officer kills whoever is in front of them, without any consideration. But keep in mind that Rambo action is for movies, not real life. Unfortunately, the expert on this training method was talking about real life – the way in which police learn how kill people in real life. Really scary training.

Mark was not killed because he was a criminal or had a concerning record. He was killed only because a police officer called her buddies to tell them that a guy was driving erratically, and without any waste of time a legion of them were ready to go hunting for the distracted driver, who was corralled and killed by a big firing squad, without having committed any crime and without any search warrant. It was hunting season for our protectors. It is very concerning to realize how easily one can lose their life on our city streets at the hands of the very people we pay to protect us. Any life is precious and should be protected at any cost, especially by police officers, whose main responsibility is to protect and defend the life of every citizen. The culture of indifference that has resulted from the high number of police crimes is also concerning. Think about the number of orphaned children, widows, and other relatives that are left behind by those who have been killed by the police. It may be time to change the laws to protect our society the way it deserves to be protected.

The Independent Investigation Unit determined no charges would be laid in Mark's fatal shooting. Shame on those people. Their organization has nothing pointing to being independent and nothing pointing to real investigations. It would be very interesting to know what aspects are considered by the members of the IIU to conclude in almost every case that police did the right thing when killing an innocent person. In this case, Mark was standing in front of many police officers pointing their guns at him, like a firing squad ready to execute a convict. The vehicle that Mark had been driving ended up with a lot of holes from bullets that missed Mark. It seems that Mark's death was an extra judicial execution style event. Shame on them.

A call for Help Turns Deadly for an Innocent Man

Craig, a twenty-six-year-old from Wasagamack First Nation was killed by police on August 2, 2008 in front of his father's house. The initial statement given by the police said that Craig was killed because he had a knife in his hand and did not drop it immediately after the police told him to drop it. However, according to witnesses, what Craig had in his hand was a cellphone, not a knife. On the day of the killing, police had received a call from a house located in the city's north end. Two women had been fighting, and the caller had asked for help from the police; three police officers arrived at the house, but the officers used lethal force before even talking to anyone. Craig, who had recently returned from work, was at the house and had gone out with his cellphone in his hand when he saw the three officers in the yard. There was a fence between him and the police officers, but as soon as they saw him, they asked him to drop the knife, which was indeed his cellphone, the police opened fire, and Craig was hit with four bullets.

The officers had just arrived at the residence, and without even knowing the reason for the call, they had already killed an innocent man, just like in other similar situations where people had called them asking for help. There was a fence between Craig and the police officers, and even if Craig had a knife in his hand, what danger did that pose to the trained police officers? Let's call it by its real name, that was a murder, plain and simple. Several years passed without any explanation to the man's family; nobody knew anything about the investigation, and despite there being a requirement for an inquest whenever a police officer is involved in a murder, an inquest was not called for at least eight years. Throughout that time, Craig's murderers continued to patrol the streets of the city like nothing had happened. The police officers were not charged with Craig's murder, and the entire police department ignored the family's request for an explanation. The indifference of the justice system with respect to this case was evident. In any other place in the world where citizens live under the same laws, it is difficult to leave a crime without justice being served, and nobody should be above the law. When a crime is committed, it must be investigated impartially, and those responsible for the crime must be charged and punished; the absence of this, results in anarchy and impunity.

The police officer who killed Craig said that after they tasered him and asked him to drop the knife, he shot him four times because he disobeyed the order. Common sense would say that his intention was to kill Craig, not for committing a crime but for not obeying an arbitrary order from someone who thinks that a uniform gives him the authority to kill without consequences. Those who are empowered by the uniform, in many cases, can be very dangerous for private citizens. It is obvious that the officers who attended the call that fateful day were empowered by the uniform. After killing Craig, they kept the rest of the family inside the house without letting them go out. After that, the shooter ordered the other two officers to take the family out of the house and handcuffed some of them for unknown reasons. The killer ordered the other officers to handcuff Craig's father, his uncle, and his father's girlfriend. This was an absolutely disgusting and shameful behaviour by those public servants acting in the name of the justice system. Those abuses may be normal only in undemocratic countries, where some members of the State live and act above their country's laws.

Ismon Marroquin

It is disgusting to learn that after killing an innocent young man, the killer committed a series of abuses with the dead man's relatives, and it is yet more disgusting to know that the whole justice system condoned that unacceptable attitude, since for almost eight years it ignored the claims of Craig's relatives. Those officers acted as though they are the only authority in place, and they are untouchable. The required inquest finally began, eight years after the killing. It found more of the same – no wrongdoing by the police officers. Inquires rarely provide anything good for the suffering people who lost a relative. Only more pain and power to the executioners. Something must be wrong in the judicial system of this country; the lack of proper authority is easy to see. People are scared and need protection from their protectors. A society does not have any hope when the foundation of its justice system is rotten.

Police Killed a Teenager and After Tasered his Cadaver

Sammy, an eighteen-year-old young man, whose parents immigrated to Canada from Syria, was killed by police officers on a streetcar. The Toronto police killed the teenager after they ordered him to drop a knife. This was all captured by surveillance cameras and cellphone videos. In an era of abundant video technology, it has become more difficult for the police to hide, frame, or cover up their crimes, it has become increasingly difficult for police officers to change the facts when they are obvious through video images. If it were not for those resources, many crimes would go without any clarification, given the police force's tendency to blame the victim for their actions.

In this case, it seems that Sammy had a knife, which the officers asked him to drop while he was on a streetcar, far from them, which meant that he did not pose any danger to them. However, they decided to kill the boy anyway, shooting him nine times. First, they shot him three times, and after six seconds, they fired another six rounds, just to make sure they had killed their prey. Nobody would believe that these officers shot nine bullets just to defend themselves, and nobody would think that to immobilize a man you need to shoot him nine times. This incident was yet another

Empowered by the Uniform

assassination by those empowered by the uniform and life goes on while these officers continue to patrol the streets until their next fatal encounter. Once they had killed Sammy, they used a taser gun on his body, possibly to make sure he was dead. Shame on them.

According to information from the media, killings by police in Toronto are quite common, and like many other police killings across the country, they go unpunished. But Sammy's killing resulted in protests with hundreds of people condemning the police actions. I wonder how those killers feel whenever they kill an innocent person? it seems like every police station is a nest of killers, which would scare those who are lamenting the killing of relatives and friends. If it is normal for police officers to kill people without a reason; I wonder how many officers have blood on their hands in this country? If more crimes are treated with impunity, it must follow that the police enjoy the complicity of the justice system; therefore, not all blame falls on the killers, but on those who are providing the weapons and other resources to commit the crimes and not prosecuting them.

Professional police officers would never need to use their pistol to kill a person, especially if that individual is doing nothing wrong; whoever uses his weapon without being attacked, is not a good police officer and must be dismissed from the force, arrested, and charged with murder. It is a discredit to the good police officers, to know that inside the force, there are people using the uniform to show who they really are, and they never will be discovered due to the fear of complicity of the good elements. I am sure that many police officers reach retirement without ever having used their pistol in difficult situations. But the natural killer takes advantage of any opportunity to calm his anger, frustrations, and pathologic instincts. They kill without remorse.

Good police officers, like any other professional, will enjoy retirement in the company of their family; but whoever retires with blood in their hands, will not have peace and will not rest, because the finger of holy justice will point to them wherever they are, alone or with their family. The Special Investigation Unit identified one shooter and twenty-two witness officers; twenty-three untouchables in total, to cut short the life of a young man. If those police officers had tasers and did not intend to kill the young man, why not used the taser first? Moreover, if the police officers are properly trained, they should be able to disarm a man without using lethal force, but if they are trained to use their pistol in any confrontation, any other methods would be useless. It sometimes feels like their instructions are to kill anybody who has the misfortune of crossing their path. There is no other explanation for killing a young man this way.

A Man Attacked by RCMP Officers Dies of a Brain Hemorrhage

Nathan was killed in The Pas on November 29, 2008, by RCMP officers who were called by his ex-wife Lorna, to help with a family problem. It seems that the officers found that the easiest way to solve the problem was by taking Nathan's life, a life that did not have to be taken. According to information provided by his family and the media, Nathan and Lorna met in Winnipeg in 1994, and two years later they had a child, Cheyanne. When the couple started having family problems, Lorna decided to end the relationship and separated from Nathan in 2001.

She moved with Cheyanne to The Pas in 2006; while Nathan decided to stay in Winnipeg. In September 2008, when Cheyanne was Twelve years old and started showing behaviour problems, her mother though it was too difficult to deal with her daughter as a single parent, so, she asked Nathan to come to The Pas and stay with them temporarily, so that he could also be involved with Cheyanne's behaviour. Nathan arrived at The Pas on November 11, 2008, and stayed with Lorna and Cheyanne in the house that his ex-wife was renting. However, the old problems soon started taking place again, and on November 28, Lorna Called the RCMP, asking them to remove Nathan from her house. While Nathan was sitting on a chair in the kitchen, Lorna went outside to wait for the arrival of the officers, but did not ask Cheyanne to go out, with her, which gave Cheyanne the opportunity to see everything the police officers did to her dad when they entered the house.

When five RCMP police officers arrived at the house and encountered Lorna outside, they asked her to stay outside while they entered to arrest Nathan. According to Cheyanne, in a matter of seconds, the officers had her dad on the kitchen floor while kicking him in the head, applying pepper spray to his eyes, holding him down with their feet, and kneeling on top of him, while others were handcuffing him. Cheyanne was yelling at them to leave him alone and stop kicking him because they could kill him; while she was yelling, an officer told her that if she did not stop yelling, they would take her too.

When Lorna came into the house, she saw that the police were using excessive force against Nathan, who had stopped moving while he was face down in the kitchen; the officers still had their feet on him and were kicking his head. According to Cheyanne, her dad was unconscious when the officers dragged him from the kitchen to the police truck waiting outside. She also heard a loud noise when they were dragging her dad down the deck stairs, something like he had fallen. Lorna saw Nathan on the snow at the end of the deck stairs. He left a pool of blood in the kitchen and another where he was lying on the snow outside the house because of the blows to his head. Instead of taking him to jail, they took him to the hospital, because they knew they had hit him too hard and he was not responding.

Dr. Kumka was in charge of the emergency room when police arrived with Nathan in a vegetative state. The doctor said that Nathan was not breathing, had scratches on his face, and was bleeding from the ears. When tests were done, it was found that he had suffered a brain hemorrhage as a consequence of the blows to his head. The next day Nathan was declared dead because of the brain hemorrhage. However, as usual, the police officers got away with murder, and all five were declared innocent of the crime. Another case in which police are called to solve a domestic problem and they leave a corpse for the family who called them. Significantly amplifying the magnitude of the problem that the family had before calling the police. It is obvious that the police arrive to help in the only way they know very well, which is killing one of the members of the family who asked for help. But if the crimes remain in absolute impunity, it is because of the accomplices that police have in the justice system. How it is possible that a crime of this magnitude would result in absolution of the killers? Who are those investigators that have the guts of ignoring the tragedy? this kind of crimes are keeping the whole system under the microscope. The first crime was killing an innocent man and the second crime was to absolve the killers by their accomplices.

Ismon Marroquin

During the investigation, the police officers said that Nathan was drunk, but his ex-wife denied that there had been any drinking involved when she called the police. In addition, the officers said that the man became combative, but the family knew that he had been removed from the home unconscious. It appears that all police officers who kill innocent people have the same excuse to justify their aggression: He was combative. He resisted arrest. He assaulted a police officer. He did not obey the orders. He had a weapon. However, apparently, some people still believe in the excuses used by the police.

An inquest into Nathan's death was conducted, and when Lorna was called to testify, she said that she was totally shocked, and while the RCMP officers were giving their testimony, the presiding judge asked several questions and later he said that the police officers contradicted each other. All five officers were exonerated in Nathan's killing, which says nothing new about the way our justice system works. The man was killed in a brutal way because the officers destroyed his brain kicking his head. The doctor who received his destroyed body at the hospital said that the man was in a vegetative state, in other words, he was already dead. It is disgusting to learn that our justice system has tolerated those crimes with absolute impunity.

It appears that the laws applied to police forces are totally different to the laws applied to simple citizens or common people. It must be the uniform that empowers them to kill and get away with murder. What would happen if five regular people threw a person on the floor and killed him with kicks to the head. Would the law exonerate the five perpetrators, or would it punish them? If the answer is that the five would be arrested and charged with murder, then we have a situation where the law is discriminatory and confirms that there is a set of laws that apply to police officers and another set that applies to people without uniform. If this is indeed the case in our justice system, then there is a huge legal problem in this country, since even in most developing countries, the same laws are applied to everybody.

Young Man Killed by RCMP with a Rain of Bullets

Bill, a teenager resident of Eriksdale, Manitoba, was killed in Lake Manitoba First Nation by RCMP officers on November 15, 2017. Some of the events are confusing and, in some way, difficult to accept, but we must depend on the information supplied by the officers and the family members who talked to him before he was killed, because there were no impartial witnesses. According to the information provided by different sources, including the media, on the night of November 14, 2017, a lone police officer was assigned to take Bill to the remand centre in Winnipeg, because of theft from a VLT worker machine. The prisoner was handcuffed and chained at the ankles before starting their trip. On their way to Winnipeg, Bill asked his custodian permission to pee, which the officer granted, but according to the police officer, Bill attacked him from behind, and a scuffle unfolded, with Bill trying to overpower the officer, who was firing his pistol over his shoulder until the pistol jammed. The officer later said that he fired his weapon more than once but apparently only one bullet hit Bill.

The Independent Investigation Unit said that the officer fired thirteen bullets at Bill, who in the end overpowered the police officer, took the pistol with him, and escaped in the unmarked police van, despite being shot once in his left shoulder. The police officer radioed the detachment to inform them of the attack and the theft of the van and his pistol. Nobody knows what was really said to the attendant who received this information, but from that moment on, a manhunt was organized by the RCMP for Bill, who was then accused of attacking a police officer, and stealing the van and his pistol.

Soon after the event, the public started asking simple questions: Why did the authorities in Lundar send only one police officer with a prisoner to the remand centre in Winnipeg? Why did the transfer have to be done at night? Why was the prisoner able to attack a police officer from behind and overpowered him if the prisoner had his legs shackled and had been shot on his left shoulder? Does it mean that during their training, police officers do not receive instruction on self defense? Is their training related only to the use of lethal weapons? Why was the police officer not able to shoot at the foot, leg, or any other part of Bill's body? If he had his hands free? What kind of weapon was the officer using to fire nine bullets before the pistol jammed?

After Bill stole the pistol and the van from the police officer, he returned to his home in Eriksdale. When he arrived, he spoke to his mom Irene, and his sisters Rebeca and Diane, who saw Bill bleeding, especially from his left arm. That was the last time they saw him alive.

Close to midnight, a police officer driving a cruiser spotted the unmarked van near Lake Manitoba First Nation and decided to follow the van. After a high-speed chase in the community, Bill lost control of the van and went into a ditch. The officer who was following Bill, asked his superiors if he could shoot a tire of the van, and the answer was no, because some officers from the Emergency Response Team were on their way. Those officers got to the site two hours after the officer had called the detachment. According to the information supplied by the officers, the five heavily armed officers arrived at the place where Bill had the van still running and was trying to remove it from the ditch.

They did not waste any time; two officers with the rifles pointing at Bill asked him to turn off the van and show his hands. Thirty seconds later, they all fired at Bill without any warning. The autopsy showed that Bill died from multiple gun shots. The events showed a clear decision to kill the teenager, who had had more than one encounter with police officers in the area, according to information provided by the police. Bill's murder was unnecessary because police should have used other means to arrest him, but instead, they did not give him any opportunity to surrender and deal with the problems in court. It is also possible that Bill was charged with a crime he did not commit, because his sister Rebeca said that the RCMP had a video showing another man stealing the VLT. She said that on Sunday, she had seen messages on Facebook accusing Bill of stealing from VLTs in the community. His sister Diane, said that she was at home when he arrived covered in blood and dripping blood on the floor, and he told her that he could not move his left arm; Diane also said that Bill was at home when the VLT was stolen and that he was receiving death threats from a member of the First Nations community, and she was sure that the RCMP had arrested the wrong person for the robbery.

The officers who shot Bill refused to give interviews; they only gave a written statement to the prosecution. When the facts are not clear, the public has the right to doubt the information received regarding people who are suspects of a crime. In this case, there are a lot of unanswered questions, but unfortunately the only person who could shed some light into what happened is dead. As usual, the Independent Investigation Unit recommended no charges against the officers who killed Bill. It is safe to ask what kind of methodology is used by the IIU to conclude that police are not at fault when there were no witnesses, or at least, no impartial witnesses? That institution seems to be so efficient that, usually in record time, they jump to conclusions without scientific evidence.

This was another case in which the only people testifying were the police officers who killed the young man. It is amazing how fast the IIU can solve a crime and absolve the killers without any forensic or scientific evidence and even without a real investigation; and they are always right because nobody can contradict their verdict. The information of the five officers with the mission to execute Bill was enough, it shows they did a perfect job because, they complied with the orders received. They proceeded with the killing, execution style, with a firing squad. Five well armed officers a few feet from their target.

It is really concerning that the police act as though they are the maximum authority of the land. They appear to have to confidence in the justice system and judges applying the law. They only trust the way they impose the law.

Community Concerned for Family of Man Shot by RCMP Officers

Paul, a fifty-two-year-old man, was killed by RCMP officers on March 15, 2011, in the community of God's Lake First Nation. According to information obtained through different providers, Paul was at his home when he realized that a group of young people were vandalizing his sister's house, so, to scare the guys away, he fired some shots into the air. After that, he decided to follow them down the hill in the direction of where two RCMP officers were guarding a house that had caught fire two days before, and where two children and their grandfather had died.

When Paul approached the officers, he started talking to them while holding the gun. One of the officers asked him to drop the gun, but Paul insisted on talking to them while he continued to walk toward them. The officer did not care about what Paul was saying and insisted on asking him to drop the gun. In the confusion, the officers opened fire, shooting Paul in the arm, which resulted in massive loss of blood and his subsequent death. The community reacted with anger toward the officers who, in their opinion, were too quick to shoot a nice and peaceful person of the community.

The victim had four children and five grandchildren; he worked as a carpenter and was a very good person. When his gun was checked, it was found to be empty, which proved that Paul was only wanting to talk to the officers. Paul's brother said that the officers were too quick to pull the trigger. Their actions make me wonder if they follow a protocol that they can not change under any circumstance, demonstrating that the use of words is meaningless, possibly because of the type of training they receive; shoot first and investigate later. It is obvious that the life of civilians, especially Indigenous people, is not worth much to some of those empowered by the uniform.

The authorities decided to carry out the inquest into Paul's murder in Winnipeg instead of God's Lake First Nation to protect the security of the officers who had killed Paul. However, with that decision they also removed the right of community members to find out what really happened during the confrontation. When they decided to move the inquest to Winnipeg the victim's family lost the opportunity to properly heal and gain an understanding of why their relative was shot and killed. The members of the community thought that the killing was motivated by racism and discrimination. Some members thought that police officers who arrive in the community are scared, and they think that they will be attacked without a reason at any time and anywhere, which is not true. Their fear is the result of their own feelings toward Indigenous people, and they do not try to see Indigenous people as normal human beings, but as dangerous enemies.

That is probably why officers do not try to interact with the community in a friendly way and why they shoot anything that moves without checking first what is going on.

Paul's killing was unnecessary. He was a peaceful man who was just trying to report what the young guys were doing to his sister's house, but the officers made the mistake of shooting him without listening to what he was saying. The whole community condemned that killing, and while they mourned the tragic loss, it is possible that the two police officers saw this as one more Indigenous person who lost his life for disobeying their orders.

The investigation concluded, as usual, that the police officers were not at fault when they shot Paul, so, no charges were recommended. This made the chief of God's Lake First Nation very upset. He stated that the community felt that the inquest was just going through the motions to satisfy the issue that an inquest must be automatically called. It is concerning that the killings of Indigenous people continue with despicable behaviour from police officers who always get away with murder. In each inquest the system accumulates lots of recommendations good for nothing because nobody is interested in putting them in practice.

A Man is Killed by Police in Front of His Girlfriend

Eric, a twenty-eight-year-old Indigenous man, was killed by Winnipeg police officers on March 6, 2020, on Sargent Avenue in front of his girlfriend, Giselle, who said that they did not have to kill her boyfriend, without giving him a chance to explain anything to them. Eric was on his way home with his girlfriend when he had an argument with a guy in front of a house; he was carrying a small machete that was seen by the man, who immediately called the police. Eric and Giselle continued walking and stopped at a picnic table, where police saw them and confronted Eric, asking him to drop the machete. He did not have a chance to explain anything because the officers started shooting at him. When he was already down, they shot him again. Those police officers did not waste time talking to anybody; they started pulling the trigger right away.

Ismon Marroquin

Witnesses said that an ambulance took Eric to the hospital, but he was already dead. The officers handcuffed Giselle for no reason and took her away. In most parts of the world, that attitude is called abuse of power. A resident of the neighborhood where Eric was killed said that she heard a gun shot at about 10:00 PM. There was a pause and then another three or four shots. When she looked out the window of her apartment on the second floor of her building, she saw a commotion on the street, with police officers around a man lying on the ground. An ambulance arrived, and paramedics took the man, but it seemed he was already dead. She saw a woman crying hysterically and the officers handcuffed and took her away.

It is outrageous and inhumane that the authorities would allow that kind of behaviour in a police department. That approach to policing is a disgrace and a shame to the country. If Eric was executed when he was already unable to move, those police officers should be charged with murder.

According to the various cases reviewed in the preparation of this book, it has become evident that there is a pattern across police departments in the approach taken by officers when they confront somebody. It seems to be common practice for police to empty the barrel of the pistol once the first shot is fired. Should this type of approach be considered a crime? Particularly in cases where the people being killed were not armed? Human lives are precious, and nobody should be allowed to take another person's life, especially a police officer, who is supposed to defend and protect people. It is regrettable that police use their guns to take the life of a person when there are many more ways to make an arrest or deal with a particular situation. It is obvious that there are many other tools police can use if they want to solve a problem without killing a person.

An employee of the pizza restaurant close to where Eric was killed, said that some bullets fired by the officers hit the glass door of the business and destroyed it completely. Also, a cola cooler inside the business was left with holes from the bullets fired. Fortunately, the employees at the restaurant were not hurt, but they were in danger of losing their lives, due to the irresponsibility of the officers trying to kill a man. To add insult to the injury, after the murder, the spokeswoman indicated that the officers who killed Eric were assigned to administrative duties, but ready to return to the streets.

The Winnipeg police homicide unit investigated the murder, which means that the outcome was already known before the investigation started. Based on previous investigations, the result points to exoneration of the killers but more officers with blood on their hands. Nothing else.

Police Killed a Man Who Needed Help

Andrew, a fitty three-year-old man, was killed by police after a seventeen-hour standoff on July 31, 2014. A team of seven heavily armed police officers surrounded the house where he was barricaded. The police officers had instructions to remove him from the house where he had lived his whole life, a house belonging to his family, including himself. He was on welfare, unwilling to leave the house because he did not have any other place to live. His siblings decided to sell the house and split the money among all of them including Andrew, but he refused to leave; then his siblings went to court to get an eviction order, and the police went to the house to enforce the court order. It appears that the police did not try to find different ways to persuade the man to leave the house.

When Andrew found out about the presence of police officers in front of his house, he barricaded himself inside. News stories on the incident reported that the police did not make any effort to talk to him, and they did not let his family intervene or try to convince him to leave. It is a mystery why police oppose a peaceful resolution to this matter that could have ended better for Andrew and his family. After the incident, police stated that they heard shots coming from inside the house, which made them respond with several shots. The man inside the house was killed, but police said they did not know how he was killed. However, when they entered the residence, they did not find a firearm. Only his body.

The police department later informed the public that homicide detectives were investigating Andrew's death, so, just like in other similar cases, the police investigating themselves led to a predictable result. In fact, after one week of investigating themselves, it was revealed that Andrew had killed himself. The Chief of Police stated that they are a very open and transparent organization, and informed the public that the team of seven police officers who participated in the standoff were on administrative leave. Where is the transparency? was the question asked by members of the public who were following the incident. The question was valid because, there had been a lot of secrets and speculation on the real cause of death. The Chief of Police was trapped in a spiderweb built by himself while trying to defend the integrity of the police officers who participated in the final minutes of Andrew's life. Many questions remained unanswered. What kind of firearms did Andrew have? Why did police not let his siblings talk to him? Did the police have instructions to end the standoff the way they did? Why was there so much mystery regarding something that the public already suspected?

As per customary practice, there will be another inquest with more recommendations. To avoid this kind of situation again in the future. It is appalling to see the way in which every murder is covered up; it is a very difficult task trying to understand the cynical ways in which the killers justify each murder with the repetitive methods of denying and confusing. Unfortunately, there are still some citizens who are manipulated with that disgusting methodology. Those are the elements the killers need to support their atrocities. Andrew's crime is kept in the impunity like other cases, but we must accept the childish explanation that police officers heard shots inside the house, they responded to the fire and when they went into the house, they found Andrew's body but no weapons and that somehow Andrew killed himself. Nobody in their right mind would accept the overworked explanations that are presented by the police, whenever a murder is committed by their members.

Police Kill Man with Depression Instead of Assisting Him

Haki a forty-four-year-old, father of four young children, was killed by police on Highway 59. The man was experiencing symptoms of depression following his niece's death in a Regina Prison while she was held in custody. While he was driving on highway 59, a family member called police and asked them to help her relative who was suffering from depression. When police located him, they followed him and there was a significant commotion because several police cruisers started following him and when at last, they were close to him, they opened fire without a reason, and put an end to his misery by killing him in an apparent standoff. Police opened fire close to a residential neighborhood. Witnesses were able to count from their house between fifteen and eighteen police cars with the sirens activated.

Everybody who knew him, said that he was a very good person and family man who ran his own business. Police officers, who are supposedly well trained to deal with emergencies, should have been able to help him instead of taking his life. His family called the police asking for help for their relative and not for his death. The ridiculous exhibition of power, using eighteen police cars to kill an unarmed man is shameful.

Officers may pull the trigger quickly because they know there are no consequences for their actions, regardless of the severity of the action. With that kind of operating practice this murder pattern may remain unchanged until the justice system changes the rules and the laws that empower the police to use lethal force without hesitation. In essence, until it no longer appears that the police are above the law.

Police Kill a Hurt Teenage Girl Needing Assistance

Eishia, a sixteen-year-old Indigenous girl, was killed by police on April 8, 2020, at the intersection of Lagimodiere Boulevard and Fermor Avenue. Eishia was accompanied by four other teenagers who had stolen a vehicle and decided to have some fun riding around. They then went to a liquor store to steal some alcohol; the staff reported the robbery to the police, and as soon as the group of teenagers left the store, police cruisers started following them.

Eishia was driving the stolen car when they crashed into other vehicles. This is when a police officer approached the injured teenagers and opened fire at the teenage driver, who was killed instantly. In any other part of the world this is called murder, a crime that is punished with the whole weight of the law. The girl was not a threat to anybody and needed help. But instead of helping the injured teens, that police officer, with the usual arrogance common to them, pulled the trigger of his pistol and assassinated the young girl, purposely disregarding the laws of the land. He must have known that his action would be celebrated by his co-workers and that he would get away with murder. We must recognize that the murder of Eishia was not an isolated case since, throughout this book, we have seen several examples where police officers kill unarmed citizens without any consequences.

It seems that police officers feel that they are members of another level of the society, and the whole system is aware of that, and tolerates them in their heinous crimes. It is true that the young girl and her friends had committed a crime, but we are a society of laws and judges, who apply the laws in accordance with the crimes. Unfortunately, it often seems that the police officers do not trust the judges and prefer to inflict punishment in their own way, sometimes by killing the suspect. It is obvious that some police officers do not recognize their place in the chain of command and think that they are above the law and the judges. That is an aberration of the justice system, and it seems that nobody has the competence or will power to fix the mess.

It is hard to understand why that police officer showed so much rage in the name of the law against a young Indigenous girl who was unable to move. Simply arresting her would have been enough to enforce the law, which in last instance was his duty and obligation. There was no need to injure more people or for the families to suffer the consequences of police brutality. Maybe he was a police officer who needed to show his authority and power, even if it meant committing a crime worse that the one the young girl had committed. The girl had stolen a case of beer, and the police officer stole her life.

The police force withheld information about the crime for four months. Nothing was said about the fact that excessive force had been used to arrest a trapped young girl, who was not moving in the car. Incredible, the IIU, after their investigation recommended that no charges be laid against the police officer who killed Eishia; what a shame, a disgrace. It is obvious that the IIU works as an appendix of the police department. How else can one justify the innocence of a police officer that has the guts to kill an injured teenage girl who is trapped inside a car, shooting her in cold blood.

SWAT Team Kills a Black Man with an M16 Rifle

Marcellus, a twenty-four-year-old black man from Montreal, was killed with an M16 rifle by a police officer who was part of the SWAT team, on July 3, 1991. The man did not even have a chance to answer any question because the killer did not ask any. According to the testimony given by the police officer who killed him, he shot the man in the head with an M16 rifle because he thought that the Black man was armed. He also explained that he did not see the face of the man, only his gestures. Marcellus was sitting in the driver's seat of his vehicle. The officer fired his rifle when he saw that Marcellus was raising his hands together, a clear sign of submission and compliance. As it turned out, the police officers had pulled over the wrong person, and the officer did not bother to ask any questions or for identification; raising his hands was enough to get killed.

This case illustrates how easy it is to die when near a person empowered by the uniform. This has become increasingly common when one is near racist police officers, who are quick to use their weapons and shoot in the name of the law without asking questions; especially given that they enjoy immunity and impunity, as we have seen in previous cases. Shooting first and asking questions later is common when police are dealing with people of colour or Indigenous people. And after they kill someone and later investigate themselves, they are cleared of any wrongdoing.

Marcellus was killed by a white police officer for no reason, except that he was Black and maybe because he was driving a nice car. The black community was outraged by the killing, considering the officer's attitude as a demonstration of the usual racism existing in police departments. Their anger grew even stronger when they learned that the authorities decided not to press criminal charges against the police officer who had killed the innocent young man. It is incredible that the officer stopped the car and shot Marcellus without even seeing his face, asking questions, or asking for his identification, despite the young man stopping as soon as he was asked to and putting his hands up to avoid any confusion on the part of the officer. Tensions have grown in Quebec because of the abuse of authority among police officers who beat and shoot people of the black community. People have asked why police kill people without asking for identification?

and why in any city are police under the impression that they are the rulers of the streets?

The politicians are the ones who set time for hunting season, therefore, they are responsible for whatever police officers are doing on the streets, because they know that they have the freedom to hunt people according with the rules made by politician who are interested in solving problems of society only when they are looking for votes. Once the need of votes is gone, they do not care about what happens when police officers are taking the law in their own hands. Therefore, it is safe to say that politicians refusing to change the laws are responsible for whatever police are doing on the streets. Any killing by police officers is regrettable, especially when they kill people because of their colour or because they are Indigenous. That systemic problem should be corrected by politicians as soon as possible, but while they are refusing to change the law, the responsibility of every murder at the hand of police officers should be shared equally by all politicians. It is a huge problem in our society to have police officers killing people without any responsibility. Every killer should be prosecuted, convicted, and sentenced to jail. Only then, will we be able to live peacefully; no matter our race or ethnic background.

Police Officers Kill a Man Who Held a Toy Gun in His Hand.

Jason, a thirty-six-year-old Indigenous man with three children was killed by three police officers on April 9, 2020, on Anderson Avenue after somebody from the house called police reporting a domestic violence incident. When the three police officers arrived at the house, they heard a scream coming from inside. When they forced their entry into the house, they saw a man pointing a gun at himself. The police went out, and a couple of minutes later Jason came out with a toy gun in his hand. When the officers saw the gun, they shot and killed him. According to his daughter, Tianna, nobody was in danger inside. When she saw the officers inside the house, she screamed because she was scared. It is sad and concerning that police officers attending the emergency did not de-escalate the emergency but worsened it.

We have learned that when police officers are called to a domestic problem, they do not always solve the problem, but create a bigger one, because sometimes they kill somebody and leave a corpse in the house. They miss the opportunity to show people that the uniform they are wearing means help, friendship, and respect and that they can be useful in those critical moments or circumstances. Too much blood has been spilled around the country by police officers who do not know how to use an appropriate approach and convincing words to help correct things instead of pulling the trigger.

According to the police, they received a telephone call about a domestic problem involving a man with a gun, a statement that is hard to believe because his family knew that he did not have a gun. The police officers mistook the toy gun for a real one and, without hesitation killed the Indigenous man. It is outrageous and inconceivable that the police officers of our city have the courage and guts to kill an Indigenous man with an AR15 rifle when those kinds of weapons are supposed to be used only by the army. I am under the impression that normal people would not feel comfortable hunting elephants, buffalos, or moose with that kind of weapon; therefore, to shoot a human being with one, must be a criminal act.

Our authorities should prohibit the use of those weapons by officers who are supposed to care for the well-being of citizens. The autopsy showed that the cause of the death was gunshots to the torso.

Taking the life of a person is regrettable from any point of view and must be avoided at any cost; and to not feel any remorse over killing a person likens us to carnivorous animals, except animals kill to eat and survive. Killing a person is a serious crime and must be punished.

Many police officers do not care about the fear, repulsion, animosity, or rejection they experience from society in general, and particularly from Indigenous people, who are placing their younger population in the hands of police officers. Their uniform imposes fear on people around them. Many people believe that when police are inside a house nothing good can be expected. People do not have confidence in the so-called Independent Investigation Unit of Manitoba; so far, that institution has not shown that their investigation is independent, because they always exonerate the shooters. If the killers are free of any responsibility in almost every case they investigate, something must be wrong with the integrity of that institution. If the IIU wants to be independent, their Board must be integrated by at least three professionals from First Nations communities as permanent members on the board, otherwise this body cannot be considered independent or trustworthy.

The Independent Investigation Unit of Manitoba said that no charges would be recommended against the officers who killed Jason because he had a BB gun in his hand. The justification is not credible. The statement of its director is shameful, insulting, despicable, offensive, and disgusting. What kind of hope can people have with and institutions like the IIU? Their members are cynical by calling it Independent. Independent of what? Independent of the interests and expectations of the public? Independent of the feelings of people suffering the shameful decisions of the honorable members that have decided to ignore the pain of relatives and friends of those murdered by the police?

Whenever the IIU exonerates officers who commit murder, its members are automatically sharing the complicity of the murder, because they do not let the justice system apply the law the way it should be applied. The judges should ignore the recommendations of the IIU because those recommendations are partial, and the outcome of the decisions is almost always on the wrong side of the law, protecting criminals and obstructing the independent application of justice.

Woman Calls Police to Help her Husband, but They Give Her His Cadaver

Viengxay was killed by police officers, after they tasered him repeatedly, knowing that he was bipolar and schizophrenic. According to his wife, her husband was taking medication, but one week before his death he stopped taking his medication and started becoming violent; therefore, his wife called the police. One female police officer was dispatched to the home. The officer had the necessary skills to de-escalate Viengxay's behaviour in such a way that, according to his wife, at the end of the intervention, both were singing together. However, one week later the sick man was refusing to take his medication again and started getting violent. His wife called the police again, but this time, the police officer who was dispatched to the house did not have any skills or the training to de-escalate a difficult situation. He did what has been done before, he killed the troublemaker, and the problem was solved.

These two situations with the same person, demonstrate that it is possible to successfully de-escalate a difficult situation without killing the individual. According to his wife, after she called the police, three officers arrived at the house and kicked the door open. Viengxay tried to prevent them from entering the house, but they entered aggressively and ordered him to sit down. The officers realized that the woman was fine and had not been assaulted or threatened; however, one of the officers kept yelling aggressively at Viengxay, who left the house in exasperation without putting his shoes on. The officer chased him and shocked him at least three times with taser guns, then they punched his face at least five times. Once the officers killed him, their job was done. But there was no reason to kill a sick man who was not a threat to anybody, especially to the "peace" officers who were supposed to help him.

As a result of the killing, his wife filed a lawsuit against the City of Winnipeg, the three police officers, and the Chief of the Police. In their own defense, one of the officers testified that he had seen through the window that Viengxay was assaulting his wife. They also said that Viengxay threatened them while running outside, and when he stopped, he assumed a fighting position; so, they threw him to the ground, punched him in the face, tasered him, and shackled and handcuffed him. But according to what an officer stated at the end of the interrogation, they shackled and handcuffed a cadaver because the victim was not breathing and was unresponsive.

Following their investigation, the IIU forwarded the results to the Manitoba Prosecution Services, which concluded no charges were warranted against the officers. It is appalling that for the IIU and the justice system, the lies told by the officers were enough to exonerate them. Unfortunately, nobody believed the trustful information of the victims and affected family members.

The power of the uniform in this country is incredible. It seems that everybody gets scared when they see the men and women in uniform. Here, the murdered person is always guilty of his/her own death because they had the misfortune of crossing paths with the rulers of the justice system. Those empowered by the uniform are always right.

If this is the way the justice system works, then when is a murder committed by police officers punishable? Is it likely that the answer is 'never'? According to the IIU, police are always innocent of their crimes, no matter how dramatic, brutal, cruel, and despicable the killing was. If three uniformed police officers brutally attack a sick and unarmed man until they kill him, is this not a crime? Would the same rules and laws apply to anyone else who kills another person under the same circumstances? Is it necessary to be wearing a police uniform to be able to act this way and be exonerated? Laws should be applied fairly to everybody.

Thompson Police Leave a Man Dead and a Woman Injured

Steven, a thirty-nine-year-old man, was killed by RCMP officers in Thompson, Manitoba, and his girlfriend was injured, on November 21, 2015; in an eruption of anger and rage, the police officer fired twelve shots at the vehicle driven by the now deceased man.

There are two versions of this incident. One was provided by the RCMP and the other by Steven's girlfriend and other people who were travelling with Steven at the time of the murder. Steven's girlfriend stated that Steven and other friends were at the bar until closing time. A total of four people were inside the Jeep. Shorty after leaving the bar, and RCMP officer attempted to pull them over, but Steven did not stop. The officer chased the Jeep in evident anger and rage over Steven's disregard for his authority. As a side note, this RCMP officer had a prior record involving anger and rage. He had been reprimanded while working in Alberta in 2011, because he chased a vehicle at 150 kilometres/hour with an evident disregard for the safety of the public.

That night, this officer decided to take the law into his own hands and chased the Jeep until it stopped on a gravel road, where the officer purposedly T-boned the Jeep, which resulted in four broken ribs to a woman inside the vehicle. The officer then approached the occupants of the Jeep, and while he asked everybody to put their hands up, he started firing at Steven, who had his hands over the steering wheel. Steven was hit by at least nine shots and killed instantly, while his girlfriend was seriously injured. It is hard to believe that this officer's actions were done in the name of the law, given his unreasonable reaction of firing twelve bullets, nine of which landed on the target of his anger.

The Independent Investigation Unit of Manitoba investigated the shooting and in a shocking outcome, found that there were reasons to press charges against the shooter. But what kind of charges? The judge found the shooter guilty of the driving offenses but acquitted him of manslaughter and other shooting related charges. The shooter was convicted for criminal negligence causing bodily harm. It is hard to understand why a police officer would be acquitted of wrongdoing after he chased a car and then fired twelve shots at the occupants, killing the driver and seriously injuring an occupant, who also suffered a broken pelvis, broken ribs, and is now deaf in one ear and has a semi paralyzed face.

During the investigation of the incident, the RCMP officer provided a version of events that was very different than that given by the people who were travelling with Steven. However, according to prior cases where police prepare statements that only they believe but the authorities of the justice system accept as trustfully, this case will be another shame on the judicial application because the testimony of the officer with a record of anger and rage in Alberta, will prevail over the testimony of the other three occupants of the Jeep where the officer executed Steven in the name of the law. It seems that the training of police officers includes an intensive course where the aspiring officers are well instructed about the way they should lie to impress the judges in case of a murder or other crimes committed by them.

We do not have to be geniuses or specialists in law to understand an aberration of the law in this conviction. It is enough to use common sense to know that this police officer was granted an exoneration of the crimes he committed. He executed an unarmed man and seriously injured a woman in cold blood; the least that he deserves is twenty-five years in jail without parole. Convicting him for driving offenses is like the conviction that many people have for driving carelessly without having blood in their hands. There is no doubt that the justice system has rotten foundations in an accelerated contamination of the whole institution. We, simple citizens do not need a lawyer degree to judge in that way. Twisting the law is the best way to keep the majesty of the corruption.

Man Chased, Arrested, and Handcuffed by Police, Later Died in Custody

Randy, a thirty-year-old Indigenous man, died in police custody on July 14, 2019, while visiting relatives in Winnipeg. He lived in the Fisher River Cree Nation, where he left three small girls. A witness saw a man jump over his backyard fence and later learned that his name was Randy. He was asking for help around 4:00 PM while police officers were chasing him. The man was not wearing a shirt and had scrapes in one side of his face; he was yelling: "help me, help me as police were chasing him across the street. The witness said that the man looked scared.

The police alleged that their officers saw a man who seemed to have a weapon; he was bleeding and walking close to Flora Avenue. They followed him, chased him on foot; arrested and handcuffed him. But the police did not say why this person had been arrested. Randy's family was clearly upset because Randy was just visiting them from the north, and they did not know the reason for his arrest and subsequent death while in custody. According to his family, when they went to the hospital to see his body, the doctors told them they could not see it because he had died in police custody and the case was under investigation.

The Manitoba Chief Medical Examiner who called an inquest into Randy's death stated that police chased Randy on foot, arrested and restrained him, which was a possible factor on his death. The doctor said that when police restrained him, he became unresponsive. The autopsy showed that he had traces of drugs in his body, and his death was ruled as accidental. However, the police chase and the restraint were factors contributing to his death. This raised significant concern among community leaders, given that this was the fourth death of the year involving

Indigenous people while in police custody. How can so many people die while in police custody? How dangerous is it to be in police custody?

To make things worse, there was inconsistency regarding the information provided to the family. According to the doctor, he did not have injuries on his body, but according to police, he was bleeding, and the witness who saw him jumping over his fence said that Randy had scratches on his face and was very scared knowing that police officers were chasing him. There were many unanswered questions that the family wanted answered, for example: Why did he die handcuffed? Why were the police chasing him? Why was there a discrepancy between what the police said and what the doctor said regarding his injuries? Those kinds of discrepancies are suspicious and should be clarified. It is becoming too common to die in police custody; somebody should explain what is going on, and why healthy people die suddenly in police custody. Any death close to police officers is suspicious. To be in the hands of authorities should be an assurance that life will be preserved not a danger of losing one's life.

Lack of English Could Result in Death

Machuar, a forty-three-year-old man from Sudan, was killed by police when he was trying to do repairs to his apartment using a hammer. He was a single man, who was still learning the language of his adopted country, which posed a significant barrier on this fateful day. As it was mentioned earlier, it is my impression that many police officers lack communication skills when dealing with immigrants and visible minorities.

Unfortunately for Machuar, he had two disadvantages, which may have been a significant contributor to his death. To make things worse, many immigrants are afraid of police, based on their own experiences in their countries of origin. The presence of a police officer can inflict tremendous stress and anxiety, rendering the individual unable to function properly. This is because of the blatant police brutality that exists in many developing countries. Therefore, the presence of a police officer may worsen an immigrant's communication challenge, particularly if they are just learning the language. Unfortunately, some police officers can not relate to this or do not sympathize with these real challenges, so instead of looking for ways to help the person in crisis, they assault or kill the person who can not express himself due to the language barrier, as was the case for Robert, the polish immigrant killed by an RCMP officer at the Vancouver Airport.

Machuar came to Canada with his family looking for a better life but had to face a divorce, which left him without his children and his wife, who had moved to Vancouver. Machuar decided to stay in Winnipeg with his cousin, who was working a night shift. The building manager accused Machuar of damaging a door, and instead of looking for ways to solve the problem peacefully, he evicted Machuar; this aggravated the suffering of the man who had lost his whole family in a strange land.

According to neighbours and friends, he was a nice, quiet, and polite person. The day he moved out from the apartment, for obvious reasons, he was making noises that some people did not like, so they decided to call the police. When the police arrived at his apartment, Machuar had a hammer in his hand, which was immediately considered a dangerous weapon by police. It is possible that the officers ordered him to drop the hammer, but because he did not understand enough English, he did not understand what the officers were telling him, he also may not have known that a hammer can be used as a weapon instead of as a tool, so he did not obey. According to police they killed him to prevent him from hurting himself or somebody else. This is a strange explanation, since getting killed is worse that being hurt by a hammer. Nobody saw the killing, but the fact is that an innocent person died in that apartment on that fateful day at the hands of the police.

I have stated before that the way in which police officers investigate themselves or through the IIU, poses a conflict of credibility, because the results are always in favour of the police, a situation that makes people think police officers have immunity and enjoy impunity granted by the system and therefore, do not care about the consequences of their actions. The IIU usually determines that the use of force was necessary; in fact, in this case, and according to information published in the media, the IIU determined that the officer who shot Machuar should not be held criminally responsibly.

Confidence in the typical IIU investigation outcome may encourage police officers to attend any call with their weapons ready to be fired. It is possible that if the IIU conducted impartial investigations and recommended the prosecution of officers who kill civilians, there may be more consideration given by police to the lethal use of their weapons. This could result in a decreased frequency of police-related killings, and maybe people would feel like there is equal justice for all.

Unfortunately, in Machuar's case, the IIU determined that the use of lethal force was justified. Machuar was dead and not able to tell his side of the story, so, the investigation relied on the only witness, the officer who killed him. According to the report by the IIU, Machuar struck one officer with the hammer, and the other officer shot Machuar many times. This statement is laughable, ridiculous, and shameful. Moreover, we can assume that the reason to shoot a person several times, is to make sure that the target is dead, and the dead do not speak and can not contradict the lies of the officers and the members of the IIU.

Whenever a tragedy like this occurs, there appears to be immediate coordination between the prosecution and police, or between the IIU and police about the investigation. In all cases the public is kept in limbo until the usual news of exoneration of the aggressors or killers is revealed. In this case, the way in which the IIU recommended exoneration of the killer is ridiculous, shameful, and childish because in the absence of impartial witnesses, the IIU decided to interview the only witness available, and it was the police officer who killed Machuar.

Another inquest with more useless recommendations took place, but likely with no action at all. There are already hundreds of recommendations that have been generated by the numerous inquests associated with police brutality, and surely this will go on and on.

Taxi Driver Killed by Police After Brutal Torture

Richard, a taxi driver from Montreal, had the misfortune of being chased by a group of police officers who responded to a telephone call about a broken window in a church on the morning of December 14, 1993. When the officers arrested Richard, they took him to the police station and proceeded to brutally assault him, destroying his internal organs, and seriously injuring his brain. He was left in a coma for twenty-nine months, at which point he died.

The incident began at 3:45 AM when Richard went to a church looking for help; apparently, he was frustrated because his visiting rights to see his son during the Christmas holiday were being denied. He knocked on the door of the church, but when nobody opened it, he took a stone and broke a window. A neighbour called the Montreal police; when they showed up, they immediately started chasing Richard as he drove toward his brother's house, who was also a police officer. Apparently, the officers had no intention of arresting Richard but wanted to punish him for what he had done to the church window. They took him to the police station where they brutally assaulted him until he was left in a vegetative state. It was reported that the police officers showed no mercy for him, after he was stripped searched and brutally manhandled in a holding cell in a police station in the city's north end.

While Richard was in a coma at the hospital, the officers were awaiting to hear what kind of punishment, if any, they would receive. When the justice system did its work, the result was 90 days in prison for two policemen; 60 days for another officer, and the fourth police officer who left the taxi driver in a vegetative state, was ordered to perform community work. Justice was served in the usual way.

Indigenous Young Man Killed by Police

Adrian, a twenty-three-year-old, Indigenous man, was killed by police officers on September 13, 2017, in Winnipeg. His mother got the information from members of the Independent Investigation Unit of Manitoba, who went to her home to inform her of her son's shooting by police during a confrontation. Police were called to the area where Adrian had been reported to have stolen a vehicle. People in the neighbourhood were surprised at the commotion from all the police cars that arrived in the area, and later they reported having heard gunshots. It was later learned that two police officers fired thirteen bullets at the suspect, killing him on the spot. As always, the subsequent investigation conducted by the IIU found the actions justified and declared the killer innocent of Adrian's murder.

This is yet another case that shows the significant division that exist between the police and Indigenous people in this city. It is concerning and tragic that most people killed by police in Manitoba are young Indigenous people, yet police assure us that it has nothing to do with racial or discriminatory behaviour. However, Indigenous leaders disagree. The CBC investigated cases of people being killed by police in Manitoba. Their investigation found that of a total of nineteen people who lost their lives in police hands between 2000 and 2017, eleven were Indigenous. The police may deny that racism exists within the force, but the numbers speak for themselves, and things will not change until officers who engage in brutal behaviour that result in death are held accountable for their actions in a material, independent manner.

The attitude of the IIU is concerning since its members contribute to the escalation of the action of police officers against Indigenous people, when they jump to immediate conclusions in favour of the aggressors exonerating them of any responsibility on a murder without a reason. A real independent investigation that may result in legal punishment for those committing the murder would bring hope to the families who have lost loved ones to the police. The investigation of every murder should be taken with special care and not exonerating anybody without being absolutely sure that the accused is innocent. That innocence must be proven and not guessed.

So far, the behaviour of the IIU seems to be partial and compromised. When police officers understand that they do not have the support of institutions that are supposed to care for the public, they will change their behaviour with people that need them, but instead of receiving help, these people are assaulted or murdered quickly and without a reason.

Police Pepper Spray a Man and Killed Him While he is Temporarily Blind

Howard was an Indigenous young man, who lived in the north end of Winnipeg when police officers shot him dead inside his home after entering without a search warrant. According to the police officers' lawyer, everything started when Kimberly, Howard's common-law wife, called the police about a disturbance in her home. When the police arrived at the home, Howard was pepper sprayed twice, once outside the house and once inside after he returned inside due to the impact of the pepper spray. The officers followed him inside and instead of disarming him while he was suffering the effects of the pepper spray, the three officers pepper sprayed him again, and shot him with four bullets to his body, to make sure that he would not pose a threat. The only witnesses to the shooting were the three officers inside the house, because Kimberly was outside with her children and another officer.

According to the law, an inquest had to be conducted into this murder, but as we have discussed in previous cases, inquests do not solve any problems. They merely serve as a mechanism to alleviate the feelings of the people affected by the murder and to hear the justifications of the killers who are typically found not liable and are free of prosecution. However, if the victim does not die and ends up injured, he likely will end up in jail for assaulting police officers and resisting arrest. Investigators usually conclude that there are not grounds to charge a police officer who killed a person. The problem is that only they know the reason for those decisions, because to a regular person, whenever there is a killing, the killer must be arrested, charged, and tried in a court of law, regardless of who the killer is. That is the meaning of an equal, impartial, and just law; however, we have seen that the law does not apply to police officers, who are treated with preference, consideration, and maybe with submissiveness.

Indigenous Man Walking Suspiciously is Killed by Police

Chad, a father of two children, was killed by police, apparently for no reason. According to the information provided by police, the media and witnesses, police saw him walking suspiciously and decided to follow him. Minutes later they saw him walking in an empty lot, where they confronted him. The police also reported that they had to shoot Chad because he was armed, although they never indicated what kind of weapon he had in his possession. They have a zero-tolerance policy that recommends and authorizes the use of lethal force when a civilian has the courage to disobey

Empowered by the Uniform

a police order, contradict any police point of view, or shows anything in their hands. This is problematic because it perpetuates the public perception of racism and corruption in some members of the police force.

Some members of the public do not trust the police because of their approach to problem-solving, where the use of lethal force is often chosen over dialogue. Maybe this approach was not a problem in the past because it was difficult for the public to learn about the brutality of some members of the force. However, more recently, technology has provided the opportunity to see the work of police, sometime in real time. The fact that people can see police actions with their own eyes may be problematic for those officers involved in brutal acts of force, since it leaves little room for distortion of reality.

According to a witness who saw everything from his home, a few metres from the murder, several police vehicles converged at the site, raising alarm due to the noise made by their sirens. Then, multiple police officers started pointing their weapons at an unarmed man who was standing a few metres from them, looking scared, like a rabbit cornered by a group of dogs showing their teeth. The witness stated that the man was frozen, doing nothing wrong and with his hands over his head. However, a few seconds later he was shot and killed by police officers without a reason. That was a murder, simply because the man had his hands over his head; it was another execution on the streets, supposedly without consequences, like many other cases.

As in previous cases, the IIU was quick to rule out any wrongdoing by the officers. This conclusion was largely based on testimony given by the police officers involved in the killing, which appears to be generally the case. Testimony given by witnesses seems to hold less weight than testimony given by those who committed the murder. One would think that the testimony given by independent witnesses would hold more weight than that given by the perpetrators of the crime. Unfortunately, this does not appear to be the case when it comes to the IIU investigation.

There are many questions resulting from this murder. For example, why can someone be targeted based on the way they walk? Why is there a need for so much back up just to follow a person who is not committing any crime? Why was there a need to shoot someone who was standing with his hands on his head? Why does an impartial force not investigate the killing? Why did they torture him mentally before his public illegal execution? Why does nobody in the justice system take care of this kind of crimes committed by public servants who take the law into their own hands?

The members of the IIU should be prosecuted and convicted as accomplices of the crime; their indignity is shameful and disgusting. They are doing a better job than the defenders of the criminals, because they exonerate the executioners before any lawyer takes care of the shameful defense. If police can kill someone just because of the way they walk, as judged by police officers themselves, everyone may be in danger, particularly if they are Indigenous or a member of visible minorities, based on the pattern observed from the previous cases discussed here. According to the witness, Chad died without having the chance to explain himself or ask any questions. Another witness stated that it appeared that the decision to kill the young man had already been made before the encounter, because police officers did not say anything to him about making an arrest. One witness stated that the officer who shot Chad, shot him until his weapon was empty.

A Killing in Good Faith

William, a forty-five-year-old Indigenous inmate under the custody of correctional officers in one of the main detention centres in the city, lost his life on February 14, 2021. His death was a mystery for some time due to an extensive cover up at the centre. The truth came to light after a long and expensive investigation, but only after the family pushed hard to know what really happened to William inside the institution that was supposed to protect him.

William was in jail accused of robbery and aggravated assault, and according to the news, there was an altercation between the staff and William, leading to his death. Officers from the Critical Emergency Response Unit (CERU) killed William, but it was covered up for almost one year, until the murder was discovered through an investigation by the RCMP. They arrested and charged Robert, a member of the CERU.

Empowered by the Uniform

William's murder at the hands of those who were supposed to protect him while in prison provides yet another example of discrimination at work as it pertains to Indigenous people. The Assembly of Manitoba Chiefs Grand Chief asked how many more First Nations people must die because of the racism encountered in these so-called correctional facilities?

An autopsy determined that William's death was a homicide. As soon as William's family heard about his death, they organized a fundraiser for funeral costs and legal expenses. The family was expecting to raise $50,000, but after several days, they had only been able to raise $6,625. Contrary to this, when the media reported on Robert's arrest, an online fundraiser was organized for his legal defense and more than $50,000 was raised in just a few days. The money came from guards from across the country, possibly in a show of solidarity for this person who had murdered and inmate. To add insult to injury, the executive director of corrections sent a statement to the staff of the centre where William was killed, saying that the staff who killed William was acting in good faith.

Police Chased a Man with Weapons Drawn and Killed Him

Matthew, an eighteen-year-old Indigenous man, was killed by city police. When police arrived in Elmwood to check the report of a robbery, they came upon a group of young men close to King Street and Dufferin Avenue; Matthew was among the group, but when he took off running, because he got scared seeing the police, two officers chased him without any evidence or proof that he was connected to the robbery. When they got to Matthew, one officer pepper sprayed him and the other shot him twice in vital parts of his body. Once he was down, they handcuffed him, but maybe he was already dead. The explanation given by the officers was that he did not drop the screwdriver he had in his hands; the same officer had said that the boy was armed with a weapon, but he did not know what kind of weapon. Witnesses closed to the incident said that they did not see any weapon in Matthew's hands.

According to information provided by witnesses, two police officers chased him with their arms drawn, ready to be fired. Following the murder, police stated that Matthew was an armed robber, but they did not say what kind of weapon he was carrying. However, his stepfather stated that police are used to shooting people first and then asking questions after the individual is already dead, and without any chance of giving their version of the events, so, the police version is the only one to inform the public about what happened. Society deserves to know the truth, especially because in the past they have witnessed a lot of misinformation, when police try to justify a murder, in such a way that they are never accountable for their actions. The unjust treatment and discrimination that Indigenous people receive from the police may be the main reason why they do not trust them. In particular, the younger generation does not trust police. They seem to fear the police, wherever they are, no matter if they are city police officers or RCMP officers. They say that both act in the same way with Indigenous people.

The public concern about the police officer's behaviour is that they do not appear to have the proper training to treat people with care, respect, and dignity; it seams like they view citizens as inferior to them, and they are authorized to use their baton, taser, pepper spray, or pistol even before talking. Indigenous people are fed up with police behaviour, especially because they do not have a way to express their concerns. Police officers are used to killing people without any mercy, respect, or consideration.

Matthew was killed while blinded by the effects of the pepper spray; he did not have to die because it had not been proven that he had committed a crime. Police could have used the batons, tasers, or pepper spray, but not the pistol. There is no excuse for killing a person when he or she is already incapacitated from the effects of pepper spray or a taser.

Many Indigenous people are convinced that there is racism in the police forces because they are not treated the same way as the rest of the society; if they were, police brutality would not appear so frequently when dealing with Indigenous people. It was known that Matthew was not part of the group found by police officers, but because he was afraid of the presence of police, he started running without a reason. According to witnesses, the young boy was just protecting himself from the enemies of his people – the Indigenous community.

The police conducted an internal investigation into Matthew's killing with the expected result. Media outlets gave an account of an external review made by the Calgary Police Service, which cleared the Winnipeg police of any wrongdoing and concluded that the Winnipeg police's internal investigation of the shooting "was open, transparent and thorough". Matthew's family decided to sue the justice system because they had lost faith in it, and nothing was being done to stop police brutality against Indigenous people. The chiefs from different First Nations communities decided to provide financial support to Matthew's family.

At the inquest into Matthew's murder, many eyewitnesses gave their version of the events, and nobody confirmed that the young man was ever a threat to police. The police officer who killed Matthew was Metis, which might reinforce the thinking that peaceful people change character in uniform, in other words any good person can be aggressive and dangerous when he or she is empowered by the uniform. It is human nature to feel different wearing any kind of uniform.

When I was running a business, I had a customer who was Indigenous and told me that he was a former RCMP police officer. He explained his personal conflict as a regular citizen and a police officer, because whenever he visited his family in his community, he was the object of bad comments and treatment from his friends and other people in the community. They all saw him as a traitor, an accomplice of the system and the people who were doing bad things to them. He had to resign and give up the uniform that had caused him much grief. His own friends would spit at him and swear at him, insult his dignity, and more. He thought it would be better to resign instead of losing his friends and the trust of the community.

Three Indigenous Men Died in Custody

It is regrettable when people die in cells while in custody. People die in hospitals but should not die in police custody. Something must be wrong inside those cells, because according to the news, three people lost their lives within thirty days while in police custody in Prince Albert. It does not matter what explanations are given by the police department. In the minds of family members something is terribly wrong inside those cells.

Police can give accurate statements, but for the citizens who remember the bad experiences of the past, their explanations will not remove the doubts, especially of family members and members of the communities of the deceased people.

In some provinces, it is possible to get information from police about deaths inside the cells. In Prince Albert, there were deaths in 2012 and 2018 and more recently in 2021; one was a thirty-five-year-old man who died in police custody on October 11 and the other was a twenty-nine-year-old on October 12. The last one died on November 7 at about 7:30 PM; all of them within a month in 2021. According to the statement given by police, it will take months or years of hard investigation to clarify what happened. Of course, that will be enough time for people to forget those deaths and only remember new ones. According to the law, every death while in police custody or at the hands of police, requires an inquest. However, the facts show that the recommendations of such inquests are not taken seriously, so they only increase the amount of information kept in the libraries of the justice system.

When people from out of province realize that those deaths are systematic issues in the province, they assume that something is wrong. It appears the public and institutions are trained to accept the information and statements provided by police in each and all cases. However, people in Saskatchewan are not convinced that everything is fine with the police, because the Indigenous communities frequently complain about discrimination and bad treatment by police forces; not everybody is happy with the work that police say they are doing for society. People remember that not long ago, during winter, police officers were picking up Indigenous people from city streets and taking them outside of city limits, where they would be left to find their way back into the city. Many of them died along the way.

Indigenous people are unhappy about the discrimination they face from police forces, and the indifference of the authorities, who do not do anything to solve the problem despite constant complaints. The abuses of police officers are common whenever members of the communities call police. They arrive to check on the reason for the call, and they often leave grief, pain, and anger behind. A more recent case was a young woman who was arrested by police officers, leaving her thirteen-month-old son with the man who is now accused of killing him.

According to her, police refused to listen to her concern about the baby when she was arrested on February 10, 2022. She was accused of being drunk, according to information given by The Federation of Sovereign Indigenous Nations of Saskatchewan. The Indigenous people are calling for the firing of the prince Albert Police Chief and the officers involved in the arrest of the young mother, whose baby was killed while she was in police custody. Police received a second call from the same home about five hours after the first one; they arrested the father of the baby and charged him with second degree murder for the death of the baby. The Chief of the Federation has accused the officers of racism.

CROOKS ENFORCING THE LAW

Two Tiers of Citizens

When a City Commissioner recommended some changes in the Crime Division at police headquarters, it was done especially because some members of that division had an evident adversity toward some journalists, lawyers, and even politicians. These police officers were doing whatever they could to affect the reputation of these people or put them in the public eye without any reason. It was a time when a prestigious city lawyer became a target, and the members of the Crime Division started harassing the lawyer until he was arrested under a false accusation of sexual assault. An independent investigation found that the real reason behind the changes in the division had been due to a plot to make these false accusations against the lawyer, who had represented the family of an Indigenous leader killed by police.

Based on the recommendation of the City Commissioner, three officers of the division were relocated, and one agreed to retire with special benefits; however, after a while the three officers were compensated with taxpayers' money. The perception of some members of the public is that politicians do not care about the conduct of members of the police force, and instead of taking strong measures to clean up the police force, those elected officials make it a common occurrence to save the skin of any officer caught in inappropriate activities. Some people think that politicians and the police force are not interested in solving the problem because there are cases in which an officer is charged for doing something illegal, and instead of dismissing him or her immediately, most of them jump to their defence. This damages the reputation of the entire force. Whenever a police officer commits any kind of crime and is not punished for it, the whole system suffers.

It was confirmed, and published in the media, that the commission hired from outside of the province to investigate the charges against the lawyer accused of sexual assault manufactured everything, and lied to the public, possibly with the full knowledge of the Chief of Police, given that he had provided inaccurate information about the four members of the Crime Division who disliked the lawyer falsely accused of sexual assault. When the investigation concluded, and the supposed sexual assault victim testified to clarify the facts, it was concluded that the police force had fabricated the crime against the lawyer for assisting the family of the Indigenous leader killed by a police officer.

The Chief of Police and the four officers were found responsible for the case fabrication and resulting arrest of the lawyer; therefore, the grievance of the police officers and the conditions to leave their posts did not have any grounds. Instead of acceding to their demands, the city should have accused them of wrongdoing and charge and arrest them. If the police force did not like what the lawyer said during the inquiry, too bad. It was his job to defend the integrity of his client, and whatever the case, the result of inquiries is typically useless, as their recommendations are not really enforced. Everybody calls for inquests for whatever reason, but nothing changes, and the list of recommendations is good only to satisfy the needs of a few people.

Through the years we have seen a lot of people killed or assaulted by different police officers, who in their defense accuse the victim of assault or resisting arrest, charges that in most cases are false or fabricated. Usually after killing a person, the officer responsible is disciplined with paid administrative leave, which is just like a vacation, while other police officers investigate the crime. This process has become so predictable that it is easy to know the outcome of the investigation before it even starts. This so-called independent investigation usually concludes that the police officer who shot and killed an innocent person is innocent of the crime. To date, despite a long list of killings, we do not know of any police officer who has spent time in jail, sentenced according to the crime committed.

They are always found to be innocent of the crime and free to keep their position in the force.

In the case of the lawyer, the officers in charge of capturing and charging him were transferred to another division, and the chief was forced to retire in humiliation. This same chief of police, in his younger years, had been awarded the Canadian Banker's Law Enforcement Medal for killing a man during an attempted bank holdup in 1971. An inquest was held into that case, as required, but as expected, the only person to blame was the dead man, and he could not defend himself. Since then, people are seeing the same or similar ways of conducting and conclude cases about police officer's killings.

It appears that there is a big hole in the justice system, which will only improve when all citizens abide by the same laws, and no one is above of the law. It appears that nowadays the law of the land functions under a two-tier system: one that applies to the police, and one that applies to everyone else. This effectively makes police officers first class citizens and the rest of society, second-class citizens. When the law is applied in that way the murder of a police officer results in immediate first-degree murder chargers, while the murder of a doctor, lawyer, or any other member of the society may result in different possibilities like first degree murder, second degree murder, manslaughter or any other. Anyway, police officers are winners and the rest of the society, losers.

A web of Corruption Involving Some of Our Finest

Thanks to a whistle blower, the public suddenly learned that not all police officers in the city were doing their job. According to the information supplied by the whistle blower, and ex-convict, at least twenty police officers were part of a big ring of break-ins in the city. This kind of news is common in developing countries, but not in an industrialized nation, where the police are deemed to be respectable and so worthy that anyone who might kill one immediately faces first-degree murder charges. Police officers are some of the highest paid individuals in the entire city. They also have some of the best employment benefits; so, one would think there is no reason to commit crimes, but maybe some of them are natural criminals and decide to commit crimes just for fun or by instinct.

The whistle blower, who was part of the ring organized by a police officer, stated that he also wanted to become a police officer himself. Is it possible that he could think that as an ex-convict, his only chance to realize his dream of becoming a police officer was to hang out with like-minded police officers? And maybe one day he could wear the uniform and be upgraded from being just a vulgar criminal to an honourable police officer. The dream might be that once this happens, he too will be empowered by the uniform. The whistle blower was introduced to the organized crime ring of police officers by its leader, who was the officer who had jailed him sometime earlier. The officer knew that his target had the required qualifications to become part of the group; the whistle blower accepted the invitation because he did not have much choice. Refusing would put his life at risk. When he realized that he would never be able to leave this group of criminals alive, he went to the RCMP and provided the names of twenty police officers, including some high-ranking officers, who were involved in this organized crime scheme involving break-ins and theft.

The criminal activities were well orchestrated by these officers. Their plan involved getting accomplices involved in their crimes and then, instead of splitting the profits, arresting them in action. Then they would sell the stolen goods and split the profit among the officers. And for the cherry on top, they would then arrest the buyers of the goods and get the goods back. To their superiors, these criminals appeared to be doing outstanding work because they were solving the crimes from the start to finish. Unfortunately, when this was all uncovered, because some of the officers had participated in more than twenty robberies, they had to be dismissed immediately, otherwise the whole department would have been complicit in the crimes.

The mastermind of the gang of robbers now walks freely on the streets. He went to university and received a medical degree or a doctorate, with pride and confidence instead of shame. Sadly, it is almost impossible to find a cure for the cancer that has penetrated police departments. Many crimes committed by police officers on, or off duty, may go undetected, and the public has no way of knowing what is going on within the force. It is only thanks to the media or whistle blowers that the crimes are disclosed. Recently, the public found out that the Chief of Police has the authority to hide information when a police officer is charged with shoplifting, domestic assault, or any minor crime. This is very problematic, as who knows what kind of crimes are committed by our finest without the public ever finding out.

Is Canada's Police Forces Getting Dirtier?

Around the country, the public is learning that many members of the police forces have been involved in crimes, the kind of crimes they are supposed to investigate such as drug trafficking, stealing, prostitution, and other offenses. Members of the police force protect themselves, and if any official investigation takes place within the force, they investigate themselves, and at the end, everything is fine. The code of silence in these organizations has become part of the modus operandi of police forces across the country; they are protected with the impunity and immunity that appear to be part of the benefits of being a member of the institution. Nobody dares to denounce anything without running the risk of suffering consequences for himself or close family members.

The corruption and conspiracy are legal and common among members of the clan. Once corruption takes hold in any institution, it is difficult or almost impossible to eradicate it. The masters of corruption know how to hide evidence, alter notes, give elaborate false statements, testimonies, instruct witnesses, or silence possible obstacles in their way to get what they want. It appears that no matter what they do, they are protected by the Association of Police in their respective jurisdictions, plus they seem to have protection from the justice system just for being police officers. In many cases, they assault citizens they do not want close to them, especially Indigenous people, as has been shown in many situations across the country, including some discussed in this book. Examples follow.

- Six police officers were disciplined in Vancouver because they assaulted three people in a park.

- In 1990 in Saskatoon, an inquiry was called after finding the frozen body of a man. A friend of the deceased saw him bleeding and handcuffed in the back of a police cruiser. In 2000 the file of his death was reopened, after the RCMP investigated allegations that the police in Saskatoon were arresting Indigenous men in the downtown and driving them out of the city to abandon them in freezing weather and without appropriate clothing. Some of them were found frozen to death.
- In Kenora, Ontario Indigenous people accused police of discrimination and racism. According to some members of the public, every weekend police officers picked up many Indigenous people.
- A man was accused by two police officers of manslaughter, despite knowing that the crime was committed by the nephew of an investigator. The cover up was denounced by a witness and released to the public.

Police Disagree with Sentence

Daniell, a twenty-two-year-old white man, was at his home when police officers arrived close to mid night on December 7, 2006, to execute a drug search warrant. He assumed that the noise at his door was due to some home invaders or criminals looking for him, so, he took his pistol to the washroom and prepared to defend himself. The intruders started firing at him, and without knowing who they were, he returned the fire from behind the door. During the commotion, Daniell heard his mother yelling at him that two police officers had been shot and a third officer was hurt in the leg due to a ricocheted bullet fired by another officer, which had passed through Daniell´s hand and hit the leg of a third officer. Since the bullet had passed through Daniell´s hand, the police took a blood sample to ensure he was not carrying any diseases.

When Daniell realized that the police officers were there to arrest him, he dropped the pistol and gave up, but the officers beat him while handcuffed. His mother and his girlfriend were inside the house when police arrived and forced the kitchen door open. Four people were injured during the exchange of fire; three police officers and Daniell himself, who lost three fingers because of the bullet that passed through his hand.

When Daniell applied for bail, the judge placed a $50,000 surety condition to guarantee his release. A curfew with only four hours a week for visiting a lawyer, doctor, or church. A ban on possessing weapons, and subject to searches of his home without warrants.

When the trial took place, the police asked for a stiff sentence, and his defense lawyer asked for seven years instead. The judge sentenced him to fourteen years behind bars, which angered some senior police officers who felt that the sentence was not long enough given that those injured were police officers. This objection indicates that there is a belief in this country that the police belong to some sort of elite group, and they have different privileges and different laws applied to them. There seems to be two classes of citizens here: the police, with special treatment as first-class citizens, and the rest of society as second-class citizens. Why is this the case? Is this ethically appropriate for a society where there is so much racism and discrimination?

What seemed strange about this case, in my opinion, is that the officers did not kill Daniell. Based on the many stories told in this book, most search warrants end with the home occupant killed by police, moreover, in this case, some police officers were hurt during the exchange of fire; the only possible explanation is that the accused was white. It is great and promising that in this case nobody resulted dead.

Police Officer Guilty of Brutal Assault

Jason, a twenty-eight-year-old man from Barrie, Ontario was walking peacefully accompanied by a friend when he was savagely assaulted by a police officer outside the Bayfield Mall in the city of Barrie in November 2010. The only reason for Jason's brutal assault was that his friend broke a Christmas ornament. After the attack, the officer tried to frame his victim, who left a pool of blood on the floor as he was attacked even when he was already handcuffed. Besides being brutally assaulted, Jason had to hear the lies of the officer who attacked him when he presented fabricated evidence to the jury and the judge. Fortunately, the attack occurred in a shopping mall where there were many people who could testify about the brutality of the officer, plus cameras recorded the entire incident. Trying to blame the victim after the attack, the officer accused him of being intoxicated, resisting arrest, an attacking a police officer, which is the common recipe used by police when there is no valid argument for their behaviour.

Those accusations typically take the form of real crimes because they are presented by a public servant representing the law in public places. When the assault took place, it appeared that the officer was in a violent rage and forgot there were cameras everywhere inside and outside the malls, recording everything that happened. This gave the judge enough evidence to drop the charges against Jason, the victim and convict the aggressor of assault, fabrication of evidence, lying, and obstruction of justice. The pool of blood left by Jason on the floor was another piece of evidence of the brutality that had taken place.

It is a shame that those officers can inflict so much pain and fear on civilians in the name of the law. A real disgrace to the institution they represent and the justice system, whose reputation continues to be at risk thanks to those officers of the peace.

Woman Handcuffed to a Table in the Police Station

Brenda, a thirty-five-year-old account manager, experienced brutal and humiliating treatment at the hands of a police officer who arrested and took her from her home to the police station without reasonable cause, just because she called for help. According to her, she called the police due to a domestic problem with her boyfriend.

When two police officers arrived at her home, they started threatening her with profanities before arresting and throwing her in the back of the police cruiser. When they arrived at the police station, one of the officers mistreated and humiliated her while he handcuffed her to the leg of a table. This all happened while she was still wearing only a nightgown because they did not let her change during the arrent. After she had been mistreated in a show of power and abuse of authority, the officers left her alone for over one hour without any explanation. Perhaps they were trying to show her that they had the power to do with her whatever they wanted.

The judge who heard the case was surprised at the brutal treatment the woman suffered at the hands of the police. They had charged her with two counts of assaulting a police officer, but these charges were later removed by the judge once it was clear that she had been the one abused by these two officers. Brenda later stated that she can not trust the police anymore.

It is hard to understand why police officers act arrogantly whenever they are dealing with the public. It feels like they immediately resort to violence instead of holding civilized conversations to solve problems.

Nobody is Safe When Police Are Around

Nowadays, it can be hard for police to deny wrongdoing when they are in action, given that most bystanders carry cellular phones that can capture an officer's every movement, and video recordings are readily accessible to the courts. The policy of denial is becoming increasingly challenging for police officers. Police officers were videotaped beating a man, a situation that angered the public. When some workers on strike at Boeing were arrested and put inside a van, police pepper sprayed them directly in their faces. Police are permitted to use force with discretion, such as physical force, pepper spray, or lethal force, understanding lethal force as pulling the trigger, something that is the first step for some police officers.

When police officers pull the trigger in situations where it is not justified, they blame the victim for resisting arrest and assaulting a police officer. They know the impact of these two rules, because some police officers assume that they are untouchable and can do whatever they want when wearing the uniform, and sometimes without wearing it. To defend their unjustifiable actions, they accuse the victim of resisting arrest and/or assaulting a police officer. They impress lawyers, juries, judges, and politicians with their statements.

When the Boeing workers were picketing close to mid night, about fifty police officers started pepper spraying everybody, according to the person who was recording everything with a video camera. When Sheldon was pepper sprayed directly in his face, he was blinded temporally by the chemicals. He was pushed to the ground, where four police officers sat on top of him and hit everywhere, including head, back, legs, and face. The Chief of Police promised to investigate the conduct of the officers, and the union officials asked for a public inquiry. We already can guess the result of both – the police always result free of charges.

Mr. Brown Cannot Drive a Fancy Car

Jackson, an African American man, knows how dangerous it is for a black man to drive a car that police may think is not compatible with the owner's colour. He had a Cadillac Catera, and one night, while he was driving his car accompanied by his girlfriend, he passed by Central Park in Winnipeg. Two police officers saw him and started following him around the city.

After mid night he dropped off his girlfriend and parked his car in the parking lot of a convenience store in the north end of the city. A few minutes later, the police cruiser that had been following him stopped next to his car, and one of the officers got out of the cruiser and started attacking him verbally and then physically, without any reason. Any answers Jackson gave to the officer's questions were met with escalating abuse. In a matter of minutes, his car was surrounded by several police cruisers and officers. He started yelling for help, but nobody got involved, possibly due to fear of retaliation by the police, or even worse, fear of being killed. Fortunately for him, the officers left without arresting him or charging him with anything like assaulting a police officer or resisting arrest. However, for Jackson this was a terrible experience, given that he was not committing any crime when the officers decided to start following him. He felt frustrated, helpless, and psychologically offended because the people who are supposed to be trusted, are the ones who insult people just because of the colour of their skin. He spent the rest of the night crying and asking himself why discrimination played such a large role everywhere in the world?

Unfortunately, there's still a lot of work to do in this country regarding discrimination; racism is a significant problem within safety and security forces. Some institutions are already working toward changing the behaviour of police officers, who in the past have been involved in serious problems with Indigenous people and minorities, however it will take a long time to cure this cancer.

Brutal Beating for a Case of Beer

Henry, an Indigenous young man, and a friend decided to steal a case of beer that was visible inside a car parked on the street. Minutes later, they were arrested and taken to the Public Safety Building, where Henry was placed in an empty cell by himself. While he was lying on the floor, waiting, one of the officers who had arrested him came into the cell and kicked him in the stomach. He then dragged him out of the cell and took him in a car to the remand centre, where he was brutally assaulted by the same police officer, who apparently wanted to kill him. The officer kicked him so many times in such a brutal way that only the intervention of some of the staff of the centre prevented him from killing Henry. When the officer stopped the brutal attack, Henry was chocking in his own blood, which was coming out of his nose, mouth, and rectum. The attack was so brutal that Henry spent two weeks in the hospital, where he had to undergo two surgeries to stop the internal bleeding caused by an officer of the peace.

After two weeks in the hospital, he was transferred to the jail hospital at the Milner Ridge Correctional Centre. The police officer who attacked Henry, and who was also the nephew of the Chief of the Winnipeg Police Service, was charged with aggravated assault and put on administrative leave. This assault is yet another example of the extent of the abuse of power by those who are supposed to protect us. That officer attacked a man for no reason at all, and he did it with the advantage of his position. He was armed, he was empowered by the uniform, and he was the nephew of the Chief of Police. His actions continue to aggravate the wound inflicted on Indigenous people by so many, including the police. If police officers are not held accountable for these types of crimes, the problem will continue to grow and will spread like a cancer, to other members of society. If police officers knew that bad actions could bring consequences, they would take a different approach with the public. That officer's behaviour deserved immediate suspension, but if he counted with his uncle's approval, then his actions say a lot about his circle.

Unfortunately, the evidence shows that officers do not have anything to be worried about, especially if they are related to the commanding officers. Assaulting a civilian without any provocation means a lot, and the politicians and the authorities should be aware of the negative consequences of those actions. No public servant should feel powerful and immune by wearing a uniform; police officers are public servants and not tormentors of the rest of the population, so, they must act politely and respectfully. They should inspire confidence, appreciation, and admiration. It is hard to hear and accept that nobody is safe when police are around.

City Police Assaulted a Man Close to Concert Hall

Flinn, a thirty-three-year-old Indigenous man, was walking alone close to the Centennial Concert Hall on the morning of June 11, 2020, when something unexpected happened to him. It seems like while he was walking around, he broke a window with a stone in one of the buildings near the concert hall. Witnesses called the police to report the incident, and police officers arrived immediately to look for the man. A video posted on social media by somebody who witnessed the interaction between the police and the man showed the public exactly what happened to Flinn when five police officers arrived one by one, and, without any discussion, started hitting him, even though he apparently did not offer any resistance to the officers.

Thanks to videos supplied by civilians, the public had the opportunity to watch the attack and saw a group of police officers kneeling, punching, kicking, and tasering the man they had face down on the ground. This time there was no way to deny the assault because the public watched the video without censorship. It was easy to see that while the man was lying on the ground without making any movement, one officer was on top of him punching his head, another was at his side hitting him with a knee, and another was pointing a carabine at him. This officer hit Flinn in the shoulder with his foot, and a female officer apparently tasered him. The officer who arrived last, appeared to be standing on Flinn´s hand. It seems like police officers are not trained to use respectful communication instead of their weapons, which they were doing from the moment each officer arrived at the scene.

The officers gave their usual report on Flinn's arrest, until the anonymous witness handed over a video showing the real events. After the assault had taken place and before the video appeared, the group of officers proceeded to give information saying that the suspect had weapons and resisted arrest. The video was aired the following day by the media, at which point, the man's assault by police officers came to light, and then the police spokesperson had to clarify that the arrested man did not have weapons, nor did he try to assault the police officers. However, while the images shown by the media were very disturbing, the police spokesperson still tried to minimize their content. To a normal person, this looked like a clear and brutal assault of an unarmed person by a group of powerful men and women, who should be held accountable for their actions. Regular people have the impression that police officers should be ready to help citizens and not assault and attack them. Is this not the right impression to have? Should one expect to be assaulted by the police for no reason and then be thankful for not being shot?

Chief of First Nations Community Assaulted by RCMP Officers

Allam, the prominent Chief of Athabasca Chipewyan First Nation in northern Alberta, was brutally assaulted at 2:00 AM on March 11, 2020, outside the McMurray Casino, by some RCPM officers from Wood Buffalo detachment in Alberta. According to Allam's information, the officers were harassing him for a traffic infraction, which did not deserve the spectacle the officers were giving to the onlookers outside the casino, where the incident took place. As many witnesses took videos of the confrontation, the public had the opportunity to watch the whole incident and come to their own conclusions.

The situation escalated as the police officers punched, knelt, and sat on top of Allam. If it were not for the video, another abuse would have been committed by those people empowered by the uniform, who have many times perpetrated crimes in the name of the law when the public could not see the real facts. Allam was arrested after an officer jumped him and tackled him to the ground, where other officers attacked him without mercy. When he was forced to stand on his legs, he had blood, bumps, and bruises on his face. At that moment, the public saw disturbing evidence about the work done by the RCMP officers, who showed no respect or consideration for Allam's position in his community. If the police can attack an Indigenous Chief with impunity, what can the public expect about Indigenous young people without any power?

In the aftermath of the assault, the officers were condemned by many sectors of society because of the unnecessary physical attack. Allam said that he was beaten by RCMP officers, and his wife, Freda, was manhandled by the same members of the police force in charge of public security. After the physical attack Allam was charged with one count each of resisting arrest and assaulting a police officer; the well known recipe of police forces. Allam accused the officers of false arrest and using excessive force.

Unfortunately, there are still some elected officials and community leaders who want to believe that racism is not systemic in policing. The fact that police officers are rarely, if at all, held accountable for their brutality makes this problem even more difficult to correct, and it perpetuates the belief that there are two classes of citizens. First class citizens are our finest, those in uniform, and the rest of us are second class citizens who, unfortunately do not enjoy the same privileges as the city's finest. If the leader of an entire community does not deserve the respect and consideration of police officers, what can John and Jane Doe expect? Allam's lawyer stated that the agitated attitude of his client was due to the systemic racism toward his people.

All charges against the Chief were later dropped, which was the least anyone would have expected after watching the video of the brutal assault. During the investigation, it was discovered that one of the attackers had assaulted another person months before while off duty, which raised concerns about this officer's violent nature. Unfortunately for the public, this officer was not suspended or removed from the force while awaiting trial. Elected officials would want the public to know that these are bad apples, and that most officers are truly exemplary and our finest citizens indeed. If this is the case, why not make sure that the apple cart is cleaned up and have all the bad apples removed? This would ensure that the rest of the apples do not become rotten.

Teenager Holding a Machete Was Shot by Police

A sixteen-year-old boy, miraculously survived after a police officer fired nine shots at him on November 21, 2019, at a 7-Eleven at the corner of Arlington Street and Ellice Avenue in Winnipeg. Following an investigation of the incident, the IIU determined that the officer who shot the nine bullets, of which five hit the body of the boy wielding a machete, was justified in his actions. There is nothing unusual about the determination of the IIU, since it appears that it is their job to justify the shootings of police officers.

The Director of the IIU said that the nine shots were not excessive in that circumstance. To me, this means that the intention of robbery is a more punishable crime than the intention of assassination by a guardian of the peace, who shot nine bullets, missing his target with four of them. According to the Director of the IIU, from his perspective, and according to the law, the use of lethal force by police officers is justified. That is enough; the officers do not need more encouragement or support; they get the message right away. However, regular citizens think that police officers should not be allowed to kill people just for fun or to calm personal rage. A civilian should never be killed by a police officer if it is not justified in an exchange of shots where the life of everybody would be in danger. The personal statement of the Director of the IIU is quite concerning and scary.

The police do not show professional preparation when they approach people who are committing a crime, especially with young people, like this boy who police officers tried to kill instead of looking for ways of arresting him and investigate ways to help him. Obviously, their only objective is to end the problem in any way possible, and the first and usually only way they find, is to kill the person. Any time police officers fire their weapons in public places, they are committing a crime that nobody prosecutes because everybody is scared. Some people live with permanent fear about police officers, including politicians and other authorities. It appears that police officers regularly use their weapons thinking that they are above the law, or at least they think that they are the law.

It is concerning that the institution in charge of the investigation has the obvious tendency to protect the police officers who hurt or kill people and condemn the victim. If the institution exonerates police, it gives approval to their behaviour and invites more of the same pattern. Every statement made by the IIU is worrisome because they do not hide their intention of ignoring the attack on the victim. How about the five bullets that impacted the boy's body? Were the bullets nutrients to the body, in the mind of the investigator? or are we talking about a human police officer and one robot without feelings? If the teen was locked inside the store, the police should have looked for other ways to arrest him without hurting him and provoking a tragedy. Instead, he ended up in the hospital, where he spent over one month recovering from the attack. When he was discharged, he was sent to jail instead of the police officer who was the real aggressor. What kind of laws are we using to convict and send the victim to jail? while the aggressor and shooter is exonerated and walks free on the street?

There is no question that the teenager was committing a crime, but we are a society with laws, and the only business of the officers was to arrest him. It was up to a judge to apply the law to punish the crime. It is puzzling why this officer thought that the best approach to solve this problem was to unload his gun on this boy, aiming to kill. A good police officer should avoid using lethal force, especially when there are several police officers making the arrest. Maybe police officers should be trained to avoid using their firearms if they are in situations where the confronted individuals are not armed with firearms. This could possibly address some of these problems. It is possible that the police shootings will go on and on, while they do not trust and do not respect the authority of the judges, whose business is to apply the law, sending the criminals to jail, while the way police apply the law is killing people who they should arrest and take them to face the judges for a trial.

Opportunity for Assault Taken by Off Duty Police Officer

Kenneth, the owner of a landscaping company, and a friend were delivering flyers in La Salle after mid night in March 2017, when the driver of a van started following them as they went from house to house. Kenneth's truck was marked with the name of his company, so, he felt uncomfortable about the harassment and tried to talk to the driver twice, but the mysterious man did not let Kenneth talk to him and continued following them.

Eventually, Kenneth and his friend decided to go back to Winnipeg, but the mysterious man followed them. While on the highway, the man passed Kenneth and started swerving his van to prevent Kenneth from passing him. When they arrived in Winnipeg, Kenneth saw a police vehicle and decided to stop to ask for help. Unfortunately, it turned out that the mysterious man following them was an off-duty police officer who, once surrounded by colleagues proceeded to physically assault Kenneth for no reason. He knocked Kenneth to the ground and started punching him in the face and head, while kneeling over him. He was assisted by the uniformed officers. This was a completely unprovoked attack for no reason at all, an abuse of power and authority.

When the off-duty officer felt that his rage had been satisfied, and the other officers had handcuffed his victim, they decided to let him go free if he promised to forget the incident, but Kenneth decided to file a lawsuit against the City of Winnipeg and the off-duty police officer. The off-duty police officer was charged and taken to court, but at the end he was acquitted by the judge. Later, the judge justified his decision by saying there had been interference from the prosecution. The public, without understanding the law but with critical common sense, perceived the manipulation of the justice system in cases related to police officers, which seemed to always have positive outcomes for them.

It is not a good sign when a judge is tempted to acquit a police officer because he is directed by the prosecution to do so. That kind of behaviour can cast a dark shadow over the justice system, particularly when the public starts to think that police officers, on or off duty, enjoy complete immunity and impunity. There was a time when civilians felt safe in the presence of a police officer in a lonely place at night. Unfortunately, that is no longer the case for many of us. Throughout this book I have expressed concern about the way justice is done, because of the excess of credibility given to police when they present statements at investigations. Many wrongful convictions have their roots in the way the police decided to drive the cases. Some police officers think that they are not representing the law, but they are the law and whatever they decide to do is accepted. This situation is very dangerous because the whole justice system could fail or collapse.

Welcome to the Capital of the Friendly Province

Nathan, a forty-four-year-old man from Fort McMurray, Alberta, made a trip to Winnipeg in April 2019 to attend a funeral and visit family and friends. At the Winnipeg airport, he got involved in an argument with somebody who then called the police. When the RCMP officers arrived, instead of de-escalating the situation, they assaulted and arrested Nathan in front of many travellers, who said nothing about the attack. After the assault, the RCMP officers decided to keep everything under cover for two months. During this time, there was no investigation to find out why the officers had used excessive force to arrest this passenger.

Maybe the case would have gone unnoticed and hidden from the public had it not been for the release of a video that was taken by Nathan's father at the time of the incident. Local media released the video two years after the attack. The video showed the excessive use of force before his arrest. The public could see how an officer weighing about 250 pounds knelt over Nathan´s neck, while another officer did something similar on his legs. The video showed the disgusting attitude of the officers, who did not care about the public watching the torture being inflicted on a man who was not resisting arrest or defending himself. Nathan was lucky to live through this incident, as he was handled in a similar way as was George Floyd in Minneapolis, when he was killed by a police officer of maybe half the weight of the officer kneeling on Nathan´s neck.

The video also showed that it was likely that the officers were exhibiting a lack of consideration and respect for a human being, along with the abuse of power, the abuse of authority, and the violation of Nathan´s personal rights. However, as it often happens, the unarmed civilian was arrested and charged by the officers with the well-known charges of resisting arrest and assaulting a police officer. Unfortunately, it also appears that the courts do little in the form of formal investigation to confirm what these officers of the peace are claiming against those whom they charge, often innocent people.

After almost two and a half years, and only after the release of the video, the RCMP decided to condemn the fact that the officer had used his knee on Nathan´s neck. They also explained that RCMP officers may place a knee on the upper body of an individual to gain control. In August 2021, the President of the National Police Federation said that their members restrain violent offenders to protect themselves. But if Nathan was not a violent offender, and was not resisting arrest, then why did the police officers assault him in front of many bystanders? Why did the police officers have to torture him if he was acting peacefully? These people will never learn. We remember the cases of RCMP killing and innocent man in the Vancouver airport; the killing of George Floyd in Minneapolis; the case of the assault of Allam in Alberta and other cases mentioned along this book.

Police Attack a South African Man

Sakiwo was a tenant in a public housing complex the night another tenant called police complaining about loud noises coming from a stereo in Sakiwo´s apartment. After 9:30 PM a camera in the lobby recorded two police officers going to check on the noise, nine minutes later they came back with Sakiwo, who was five foot eight inches and 150 pounds. He was in handcuffs and escorted by an officer about five feet ten inches and 240 pounds, who complained that Sakiwo assaulted him. This supposed assault gave the officer reason to charge the man with obstruction and assaulting a police officer, when the camera clearly showed that the officer had assaulted the man, who showed signs of being attacked on his face. Sakiwo was assaulted in the lobby, just outside the building, and behind District 6 station; his left eye was swollen shut after being hit by the officer´s fist. As the man was handcuffed behind his back – it was easy to assault him and impossible for him to assault the officer. It is obvious that in this case the officer showed racism; displayed an abuse of power, abuse of authority, and false charges against the man, who filed reports with the police service and the Law enforcement Review Agency (LERA).

After the case was investigated, the Crown laid charges against the officer. The complicity of the police department with each of its members was evident, because as soon as the officer was suspended without pay, other officers decided not to show up to work as a demonstration of their support. Do not forget that every police officer enjoys full impunity and immunity as part of their benefits. It is concerning that in many arrests made by police, the person arrested is attacked physically by the officers making the arrest. In addition, the arrested person is charged with resisting arrest and assaulting a police officer, charges that are without base as can be seen in the video but affect the record of a peaceful citizen.

The officers always win because they assault, hit, humiliate, handcuff, denigrate, arrest, and charge a person they know is innocent, without any legal consequences for them. In addition to assaulting the person, they lie when reporting the incident, adding that they were assaulted. With all their lies they can cheat a judge but if the judge does not fall in their trap and decides to imposes a sanction on the officer, colleagues immediately support the officer's actions against the assaulted civilian. Therefore, police crimes are rarely considered by the authorities.

Off Duty Officers Accused of Ramming a Car and Assaulting the Driver

The arrogance and abuse of authority is seen in every corner of the city, and at any time. Two young women driving peacefully on a city street were harassed by two off duty police officers, who happened to be husband and wife and had only been in the service for one month. However, it is evident that they already knew their privileges and impunity. If prosecuted, maybe they would be suspended or taken off street duty for a few days; but in the end, nothing would happen to them.

The two offended young women stated that they were chased on the Perimeter Highway and their car was sideswiped twice by the occupants of a Honda. The driver of the Honda was a woman who tailgated the women and after passing them, slammed on the brakes to provoke an accident, which eventually ended up occurring. The young women were fearing for their lives, because they did not know what kind of people were harassing them. When both cars stopped, the driver of the Honda got out and approached the young woman; she was screaming obscenities. She then removed the keys from the ignition and dragged the woman by the hair. Only then did the assaulted women knew that they were being assaulted by police officers, but only the man showed a badge. The assaulter took both women's purses and aggressively started going through them, looking for identification. After that she wrote her name on a piece of paper, along with her driver's licence number, and her employment's place, and handed it to the assaulted driver. The occupants of the Honda drove away, taking with them the keys of the other vehicle. Both had only been in the force for one month, but they were already showing the kind of officers they would become. With police officers like them, we do not need criminals on the streets.

The assaulted women decided to file a complaint with the Law Enforcement Review Agency against both police officers (husband and wife). Everybody has a vocation. When a person is happy with his/her job, they show excellent performance everyday, which is highly beneficial for them and for the organization receiving their services. The same situation happens when the person is self employed; it is easy to see when a person has a happy life. When a person is unhappy with their work, they are always doing inappropriate things.

According to the media, both officers had graduated at the same time and had not even been in service for a year, but their attitude was already despicable. In a simple example, both showed what society can expect from them. They are the kind of police officers that inspire lack of confidence, and one worries that during their career they might kill a person without remorse. They proved that they already have skills for the job and that they will enjoy their work in their own way.

Ismon Marroquin

Acquitted Man Sues the Police Over Brutal Assault

According to Scott, two police officers assaulted him in a parking lot of a Burger King, in such a way that they did not leave any part of his body without scratches. It was not enough for them to assault him in the parking lot, but they also assaulted him inside the cruiser and at the Public Safety Building. According with his lawyer, he was unable to move after the assault of the police officers, they left every inch of his body with bruises. Their work was despicable and brutal. It seemed like a train had passed over his whole body.

After the officers had grinded Scott´s body, they charged him with two counts of assaulting a police officer. It is disgusting to know that the justice system accepts that kind of excuse and believes the police when the assaulted person can not even move from the beating. What kind of society are we living in? Why does our society allow those abuses to happen without asking for punishment of the real criminals. Why do we accept that the police can destroy the body of a civilian in the name of the law? What kind of laws do we have? Those police officers are shameless criminals, who think that they are the law, the maximum authority in the country, that everybody must respect them and obey them like slaves. Those guys do not have dignity and have no respect for the rules of society. They can assault anybody without any worries for the consequences of their attitude. Wherever they are, they are ready to hurt or kill people whose lives are worthless according with their criminal minds.

Scott was acquitted of the charges because he had not done anything wrong. It would be a disgusting situation if the court had been impressed by the lies of the two police officers. But justice was not served, because the officers should have been charged for aggravated assault and convicted like anybody else. Clearly the court protects the police, who seemingly can assault civilians without consequences. It is sad to admit that the justice system does not apply the law in the same way to everybody. This is why police can get away with murder. The abuses the police officers committed against Scott were unacceptable and provocative. After the brutal assault, the proud ambassadors of the law, charged him with the infamous crime of assaulting a police officer and/or resisting arrest and the judges allow those liars to get away as heroes. This is a shameful situation for society, knowing that the elected and unelected authorities are not applying the laws equally, but in a discriminatory way; the law should not be subject to interpretation but applied with justice.

Police Pepper Spray an Epileptic Man Inside an Ambulance

It is incredible, inhumane and a serious crime to pepper spray a person while he is suffering an epileptic seizure. Through the media, the public was informed that police officers from Regina pepper sprayed a man while he was in an ambulance going to the hospital. The sick person was an Indigenous man, who had a seizure while being transferred to the city hospital. According to the chief of the police department, the man had a seizure inside the ambulance. So, the police officers, instead of assisting him pepper sprayed him, which undoubtedly accelerated the man's death. It is disgusting how Indigenous people are treated by some police officers. The scary thing is that the justice system did not do anything with the officers who committed the assault.

There will be an investigation conducted by police officers, maybe led by one of the officers accompanying the sick person. It would be good for the public to know the results of the autopsy, and the police officers involved must be punished for using a dangerous weapon against a person who needed medical assistance. Ignoring the crime is an invitation for police to attack citizens, and especially Indigenous people, who already experience a high level of discrimination. It is scary to know that a relative could be going to the hospital in the care of a police officer who would use pepper spray instead of oxygen to help them.

What has happened with the authorities in this country? Is everybody happy with what is going on? Is everybody aware of the illegal activities of some members of the police forces? In other countries when a police officer kills a citizen, the officer is arrested and charged with murder. After a real and impartial investigation, it is decided whether the officer is to be convicted or exonerated. This approach is a deterrent to unjustified and frequent killings by police.

Working Mother Killed by Drunk Off Duty Police Officer

Crystal, a working woman with three children living in East St. Paul, Manitoba, was killed by an off- duty police officer in February 2005. From the moment Crystal was killed by the apparently drunk officer, the entire machinery of impunity and corruption started working in synchrony. Nobody cared about the dead woman or her family; everybody was concerned about the safety and personal security of the intoxicated man. They needed to make sure that no matter what happened, the fellow officer would walk away free of any charges.

Crystal was killed instantly when Derek, the off-duty officer, hit her car from behind when she was waiting at a red light. All of Derek's co-workers and the justice system colluded in a strong cover-up; the only thing they did not do was testify that the dead woman was driving in reverse when the pickup truck smashed her vehicle. The coverup started with police officers from East St. Paul and a police department whose chief, Harry, was considered to be a corrupt officer. He also attended the accident scene and put himself unconditionally on the side of his friend, giving the necessary instructions to his officers to do everything possible in favour of Derek. The officers conducted an accident investigation in fifteen minutes, with instructions from their chief to keep Derek from going to jail, even though, they charged him with impaired driving causing death, dangerous operation of a motor vehicle causing death; criminal negligence causing death, and refusing a breathalyzer. From the beginning of the investigation, Harry was determined to help his friend and as such, he did not conduct a breathalyzer test, neither did he take blood samples because he knew that that evidence could be crucial to convict his friend in a court of law.

According to a prior investigation reported by an RCMP officer, there were all kinds of problems at the East St. Paul police department, which had turned the entire department into a cave of corrupt officers, starting with their chief. It was, therefore, no surprise that when the police

Empowered by the Uniform

knew one of their own was responsible for Crystal's death, they put the sophisticated cover up machine in motion and accepted Dereck's refusal to provide a blood sample and take a breathalyzer test. That way when the investigation got underway, the prosecution would have to drop charges related to drinking and driving, although it was known that Derek and some of his co-workers were drinking through the night, which was the reason for the accident that killed Crystal.

During the investigation, Crystal's family faced all kinds of difficulties and obstacles trying to get justice and to make Derek take responsibility for Crystal's death. After fighting for two years, Derek plead guilty to dangerous driving causing death. It was later learned that the defense lawyer and the lawyer for the prosecution had jointly recommended a two-year conditional sentence, meaning that the justice system had failed the mourning family and accepted that Derek could get away with murder, without considering the pain and suffering of Crystal's family. In simple terms, the justice system colluded for one of its own. When many steps of the justice system fail, there is always the hope that somewhere, somebody will be different and will apply justice in the right way; however, for the Taman family, the entire system collapsed when their last hope failed them. The judge's decision hit the family hard.

The next day the province called for an inquiry, as if that would remove the anger the family felt or bring their loved one back. The inquiry determined nothing new, because it was explained that Harry had given false testimony and was sympathetic to Derek, always acting in bad faith. Harry was charged with perjury and obstruction of justice, which says a lot about a chief of police, and even with all those charges, he had the audacity to plead not guilty. A police officer with a dark past or symptoms of corruption can never become a good police officer and if the masters are rotten, what can be expected of the pupils?

Video Tells the Truth about a Police Officer Beating

Eltah, an immigrant from Sudan, living in Vancouver, was brutally beaten by two police officers for no reason. In their report, the two Vancouver officers wrote that he resisted arrest and tried to disarm one of the officers, but a camera on the street told the whole truth; the camera showed the moment when the officers walked to the innocent man and without a reason started assaulting him. It is disgusting to realize that two police officers – the so-called peace keepers – can brutally assault an innocent man who is minding his own business without any provocation or exchange of words. And to make things worse, the poor man did not have any place or authority to go to denounce the attack, because the assaulters assume that they are the law given that everything they do remains in absolute impunity.

It is time that police spokesmen stop lying on behalf of the institution. It was this type of lies that led the spokesman of the RCMP to take his own life in Robert's case, the man killed by police officers at the Vancouver airport. It is disturbing and disgusting to learn that after the police officers assaulted the man, they charged him with assaulting and disarming a police officer, obstructing a police officer, and resisting arrest. This seems to be the untouchable recipe in attacks against and arrest of civilians, that is, if there are no cameras around, or judges who are easily convinced by police reports. Nowadays, the police must be careful, because almost everybody has a camera and can record disturbing beatings or brutal attacks that in the past could have been hidden from the public.

Police Should Get Criminals, Not Create Them

It is well known that police officers must comply with a daily quota of traffic tickets, and while it is easy to get a ticket for speeding, drinking and driving, driving erratically, or even for having the cellular phone with a dead battery on the passenger seat, the police also ticketed a senior who did not even own a cell phone.

Laszlo and his wife were driving on Portage Avenue returning from lunch when they were stopped because the officer thought they saw him using a cellular phone when they were seven to eight feet from his van. The officers also added that the driver did not stop when they tried to pull him over, so, they followed him and gave him a ticket for speaking on a cell phone while driving. Laszlo assured the officers that he was not using a phone because he did not know how to use one nor did he own one.

This case turned very interesting because the officers insisted that he was talking on the phone, an assertion Laszlo denied firmly. He received the ticket but assured them that he would fight it in court. Later Laszlo stated that while he does not care about the ticket, he cares about his honour and reputation, which the officers were challenging. He felt denigrated and angry at the accusation of lying to the public, something that is not part of his personality, and he stated that it was the officers who were lying.

Many citizens believed Laszlo because they had had similar experiences with the police. Many people believe that the police have the support of the justice system, and a regular citizen can not undermine the statement of an officer. In his defense, the accused man said that he did not have anything to worry about. Sometimes when people are driving and a police cruiser turns on the siren and lights, they do not know right away if it is meant for them. By the time they realized they needed to pull over, they may have already covered three or four blocks. Laszlo's wife said that after the incident was publicized by the media, she spent two long days on the phone, talking to people from all parts of the province offering support and advising them to not give up. Some of the people shared their experiences with the police, when they were unjustly ticketed, so an officer could meet the quota; this is a disgusting situation, as most citizens work long hours for little pay to be able to support their family. As reported in many cases along this book police officers lie many times when they are preparing a report for their superiors; of course, they do not expect to be caught in their lies, but technology has changed many things and therefore, there is always someone watching what police are doing on the streets and other public places.

City Police Fail to Notify Watchdog About Injuries

According to social media reports, an Indigenous man was seriously hurt by an off-duty police officer with a lengthy history of abuses. The assault was kept secret by the Winnipeg Police Service despite being required by the law to inform the Independent Investigation Unit whenever a police officer is responsible for any injury of a civilian. Five months passed until the IIU became aware of the case by accident.

While off-duty police officers are not to be carrying weapons with them, according to the information obtained, the officer in question had a baton with him when he decided to follow a shoplifter from a liquor store up to his residence. Upon confronting the man, the off-duty officer proceeded to hit the young Indigenous man with his baton and knocked him unconscious. Once he fell to the ground, he was arrested. If the police department does not respect their legal obligations, what can the public expect? Regular citizens are at risk of being treated with abuse and absolute indifference whenever they complain about concerns with police officers. The lack of respect by the police is the seed that keeps giving rise to terrible feelings between the police and civilians. It is unfortunate that some police officers with a bad record are damaging the good reputation of the department; however, it is the responsibility of senior officers to take the right measures to remove the cancer in the institution. The force is being discredited because a few so-called bad apples, that are allowed to stay with the force. If senior officers know what the root of the problem is, why are they afraid of removing, dismissing, and charging the bad officers for the good of the whole institution?

Not long ago, after an investigation into the relationship between the Winnipeg Police Service and the IIU, it was discovered that the lack of cooperation was because the police service was always protecting their officers, who committed criminal acts in a systemic coverup inside the institution. Many investigations are botched, faked, or altered, and ignored. Sometimes complaints just disappear. For that persistent violation of the law and lack of collaboration, the IIU took the WPS to court to force them to comply with the law and provide documentation that was essential to investigate some hot cases about crimes committed by police officers. The public can not be happy when the public's protectors have hidden vital information about their work or when somebody hides information or physical evidence.

The corruption inside the institution is so extensive that it is almost impossible to find a cure for the police force. Police officers have been known to commit many crimes, including theft, assaulting other police officers, resisting arrest, assaulting peace officers with a weapon, assaulting civilians, stealing liquor, wrongful arrests, discharging tasers without need, threatening suspects, destroying videos and photos, and who knows what else. But nobody has had the guts or moral authority to discharge them. The officer who hit the young Indigenous man while off-duty had also committed other crimes. With that type of background, who would like to be close to him when he is working or off-duty? Would any citizen trust that police officer to protect them in an emergency? However, this officer enjoys the confidence and protection of the Winnipeg Police Service and the Winnipeg Police Association.

Four Police Officers Assaulted a Family in a Hotel Room

Andrew and his wife Olga, decided to have a nice family evening after Christmas in 2014, so they rented a downtown hotel room on December 26, and took their children with them: eighteen-year-old Kyra, sixteen-year-old Kyuss, and Kyra's eighteen-year-old friend. Together they started the night talking, drinking, smoking, eating, and having fun at the swimming pool. Some other customers complained to the management about the noise that the family was making in the hotel, plus saying that they were knocking on the doors of other rooms.

The police were called, and when four officers arrived at the hotel, they went to the room occupied by Andrew and his family and entered it illegally. Then they assaulted Andrew, Olga, and Kyra. When one police officer pushed Kyra onto a table, Olga complained to the officer who pushed her daughter because she was pregnant. The officer struck Olga's face with his closed fist two to four times with such violence that he cut her lip and fractured her nose. Her face was so swollen that she could not open her mouth for a week. As a result of the attack, Olga lost consciousness.

Andrew was hit in his eye with a closed fist. It was swollen and pink after the attack. The officers confiscated everyone's telephone to cover up their crime, and they arrested Andrew, Olga, and Kyra for allegedly assaulting a police officer. Kyra was imprisoned for a few hours. The four police officers had to face an upset judge who was straight with them, unliked other judges who had been lenient and tolerant of the reproachable attitude of officers who committed a crime against people of different social conditions. This was one of the few times a judge rejected the systemic lies of the members of the police forces. After reviewing the footage of the video, the judge got very upset with how the officers tried to cover up their actions. It was obvious that the members of the family were innocent victims. The officers had fabricated a story.

One month after the attack, the family filed a complaint about the officers' conduct with LERA, which on July 19, 2017, said that the evidence indicated that the officer was assaulted by Olga and Kyra, contradicting the judge who saw the video footage. That is normal for the so-called independent institutions investigating complaints against police officers. The judge said that the police report and their testimony were totally different. The officers were ordered to pay damages of more than $97,000 to Olga, Kyra, and Andrew; moreover, the family won a lawsuit against the City of Winnipeg and one of the police officers. The prosecutor decided not to charge the officers with perjury because there was a reasonable likelihood of not getting a conviction if the matter went to trial.

EPILOGUE

In an organized society where its laws have worked for decades or centuries, it is expected to see that things work well, and everything is fine given that citizens are apparently happy with the status quo. However, those citizens could be discontent in some ways. The system might be doing whatever it wishes with the unhappy segment of society, but nobody dares to say anything for fear of attack. That kind of situation can polarize a country, giving way to permanent conflicts, which can increase with the wrongful convictions or the killing of people by the police forces.

With the confidence that we live in a free and democratic country that recognizes and promotes the most sacred privileges of free speech and uncensored writing, I decided to write this book, which I expect will be useful to change, improve, or eliminate, some of the most common problems that prevent a normal relationship between the authorities and regular citizens. This book addresses the most relevant cases of wrongful convictions and the old hostility that still exists between police officers from different forces and Indigenous communities, as well as members of visible minorities, which have lately increased significantly.

The lack of understanding between the actors of the different events, keeps a permanent fissure among them, which instead of improving with time, is deteriorating in a way that makes it almost impossible to attain a lasting reconciliation. This book examines some relevant cases with social implications in which the law was applied in controversial ways to convict innocent people, and where different actors of the justice system were manipulated to get convictions in bad faith. This book exposes some cases in which some dishonest and corrupt lawyers used the law as an instrument to do a lot of damage to individuals who were convicted for crimes they did not commit.

On the other hand, the systemic killings of innocent people by members of the police forces are a real concern; some police officers kill people without giving them the chance to discuss anything or explain their situation. In some cases, people who were killed, did not have to die; they were simply at the wrong place at the wrong time. Sadly, it was discovered that in some cases there was collusion among investigators, police officers, prosecutors, juries, and judges, who twisted the law on purpose to convict innocent people and sentence them to long imprisonments. Hoping to help find a point that reveals the ways in which the law was broken, and the complicity of the justice system that let the guilty go with absolute impunity, the destroyed confidence in the police force, and the chance to build permanent reconciliation, seems to have been lost.

Some suggestions are considered vital to change the behaviour of each person or group in society, and in writing this book, I honestly intend to help find a permanent solution so we can live in harmony. I hope I do not become another statistic for telling the truth, opining, and touching sensitive nerves. And while I recognize that the police forces are necessary in any organized society, it is also reasonable to expect that those forces are properly trained to engage in positive interactions with the public; if they are not trained to serve and respect the population, the result is disastrous because it could create a social problem if they commit more crimes than they try to prevent. The police forces should be respectful, polite, and well instructed, otherwise, even with the best intention to find points of agreement, it will not be possible, and there will be a permanent and increasing discontent toward the forces.

Some people believe that police officers belong to a different rank of society, which is not true. It is important that lawmakers correct the law to make sure there is no confusion about the place police forces occupy in our society, given that the law must be equally applied to everybody. Justice for everybody must be strong, efficient, fast, accurate, and without political influence or ideologic tendency. Everyone's life should be respected above all else; life is precious and does not repeat itself, so it must be respected. Whoever takes the life of a person must pay for their crime without any consideration or privileges; it is the lawmaker's responsibility to make sure that the principle of the law is equal for every person. Nobody should be above the law. The police must be respectful and considerate, and never take justice into their own hands. Whoever breaks this rule, must pay the price. It is also the lawmaker's responsibility to be sure that the law is not discriminatory. The right to life is sacred.

I am strongly opposed to the killing of people by any member of the security forces, because life is sacred and nobody should feel free to destroy or take the life of a person for any reason, especially when the killer is a member of the institutions created to control and maintain the peace, harmony and good relations of society. Police forces were established to provide a permanent sense of security in society, not fear. During the research conducted for this book, I found that many people are afraid of police officers, because when they are supposed to help, they assault, attack, and even kill the person in need. Nobody should lose their life at the hands of authorities, and nobody should be afraid of the police.

Unfortunately for many years, crimes have been committed by some members of the police forces, and the perpetrators have not faced prosecution as a regular citizen would. That is a huge problem in society and a big gap in the law, because when people lose confidence in their judges, the whole justice system is destroyed. If a person does not have the fair chance to prove his innocence, it is easy to commit an injustice. But in a fair legal process, all parts are satisfied, and if a person is found guilty, they should go to jail to pay for their crime, but not to a cemetery because a police officer decided to take the law into their own hands confident that the system would protect them. Any police officer who kills a person in any circumstance should go to jail and face a trial and be convicted like any member of society. If this does not happen, something must be wrong with the justice system of this country.

The permanent state of anger and frustration of Indigenous communities my be partly because some police forces are killing their members without reason. Sometimes the police fire their weapons to kill a person and in most cases without exchanging any word with the killed individual and leaving the whole incident in the most disgusting impunity. Police forces should review their protocols when facing people in difficult situations, because if the case is serious and requires the application of force, there are different ways to avoid killing a person. Police officers usually work in groups; therefore, they should be able to subdue a person without fatal consequences.

Police should never use their weapons just because they assume that a telephone, a plastic toy, a screwdriver, or a hammer the person has in their hand is a pistol or rifle, presenting immediate danger to the officers. That is wrong thinking and an excuse to kill the person. That is police incompetence, showing a lack of appropriate training and acting in bad faith against the targeted person. Police should think that if the person has something in his hand, it is because he or she was working. When police officers give an order, it should be clear, and they should then wait for the person to process the order in his mind and comply.

The only case in which police should use their pistol is when they are under a real attack and must respond to the fire; otherwise, there is no excuse to kill a person. If there is a murder or killing, call the police attitude by its real name – murder, killing, or assassination; and the consequences should be the same as those applied to civilians. Taking the life of a person in cold blood is a murder, simple. No police officer has the obligation to kill a person to comply with their job, because if his superior gives the order to kill a person without a reason, the officer should tell him respectfully but strongly, that he will not kill anybody while doing his job, and if that is not accepted, resign from that work, and keep your soul clean and in peace. Think for a minute how people who have lost a relative for no reason, to the police, must feel. And if you are a police officer, think what your children and spouse must think and feel about the blood you will carry permanently on your hands if you kill someone. Police officers are not killers; they are peacekeepers.

It is concerning that politicians in charge of making the laws are silent about the behaviour of some police officers with evident bad intention to kill or compromise the safety of a person. In wrongful convictions, the injustice usually starts with the police officers investigating the case, where they hide, change, or manipulate evidence with bad intentions. In those situations, they should be penalized to improve the whole justice system and avoid injustices. To make matters worse, that kind of behaviour guarantees the twisting of the law in favour of the guilty officers.

Often, cases were planned from the biggening to negatively impact the defense's chances to gain the freedom of their client, who after a long path and hard sacrifice could prove his innocence. To make things worse, the conspirators also presented false witnesses and tried to manipulate members of the jury to get a conviction, which is hard to reverse due to the slow process of appeals. There was a case in which the file was kept inside the drawer of the desk of a high-ranking authority for ten years, waiting for the papers to be signed while the wrongly convicted person rotted in jail. That is a horrendous monstrosity by the justice system. Shame in those people.

This country champions the respect of human rights, so, it should be careful with the injustices committed against its own people by prosecutors and investigators, who in some cases put people in jail to suffer on purpose, from false accusations, which result in wrongful convictions, as was shown along this book. Police officers who do the investigation with the approval of prosecutors, have the freedom to do their work without proper supervision, so they can accommodate the investigation in a right or wrong way, since nobody fears any personal consequences. Something similar happens when a police officer kills a citizen; the investigation is often tainted from the beginning because it is conducted by other members of the same police department, or by the IIU. The IIU has proven many times that it does not have anything independent about it; it appears to be an appendix of the police forces given that in most cases, the investigation seems to be partial and not credible. Usually, the investigators are satisfied with the statement given by the same police officers involved in the crime, and they prepare their report, stating that the shooting was necessary, inevitable, and legal. Those statements make the IIU fragile, inconsistent, and tendentious. They almost never assign any kind of blame to the officer, usually just recommending a minimum sanction. The blame is always put on the dead victim. If that institution does not change its behaviour, it will continue to lose the confidence even of people close to the police forces.

In each of the cases discussed here, the IIU served the interests of the police officers; they immediately jumped to conclusions without any supporting forensic evidence. In addition, they never mentioned the percentage of blame carried by the officer who pulled the trigger, which encourages these officers to continue to act in the same manner for years. Therefore, that institution can not say that its work is independent; it seems to be a branch of the police departments, doing what they are ordered to do in favour of the officers implicated in a murder.

To do a real independent and credible job, the Board of Directors should be comprised of people from different social status or groups, including two Indigenous lawyers, two Indigenous women, two professionals of colour, two retired police officers, one retired judge, and the rest like it is formed now. In addition, officers should never be exonerated too quickly, whether the killing was reasonable or not. Every officer who commits a murder should go to jail until it is demonstrated that his actions were justified, and then freedom can be regained under some legal conditions.

Another potential deterrent to police killings is to compensate each member of the victim's family with one million dollars. If the deceased did not have a spouse or children, the money should go to the parents. And all this money should come from the police budget. Consequently, every killed person will have a price, and no police officer will be willing to pull the trigger and risk going to jail and being in trouble with the law, his job, and society. However, nothing will work if there is no cooperation and direct intervention by the people in charge of making decisions: lawmakers, lawyers, judges, and politicians. The actual laws controlling the police forces and detention centres must be changed, because if the laws, statutes, rules, and protocols do not change, nothing else will change. All those people have turned a blind eye to the multiple killings and wrongful convictions.

We have learned that in some cases the investigators have acted maliciously, altered information, lost vital information, contaminated evidence, corrupted witnesses, and hid vital information from the defense. The lawmakers must legislate in favour of automatically compensating the family of a killed person by any police officer. In the short, medium, or long term, the effects of this intervention will be seen by society as a huge improvement of the justice system and safety of the public. When the authorities work in favour of the people, everybody will be a winner.

REFERENCES

Jury finds Milgaard guilty. Saskatoon Star Phoenix. January 31, 1970.

Determined mother vows to clear so's name. Winnipeg Free Press, February 28, 1991, Pag 12 By Terry Weber and Bruce Owen.

Public Airing Vowed of federal bungling. Winnipeg Free Press. February 28. 1991, Pag 1. By John Douglas.

Milgaard reads verdict in friend's pained faces. Winnipeg Free Press March 13/ 91, Pag 1 By Dan Lett.

Constable no crook, lawyer tells court. Winnipeg Free Press September 17, 1991.

Three more constables suspect in B and E ring. Winnipeg Free Press, September 17, 1991, By Paul Wiecek.

Vindictive police handcuffed woman to table. Winnipeg Free Press. February 13, 1992, Pag A1 By Sharon McKay.

Judge flays vindictive police. Winnipeg Free Press. February 13, 1992, Pag B17 By Allison Bray.

Milgaard Commission Releases Final Report. Democratic Governance. October 9, 2008. By Natasha Dube.

Whistleblower alleges 20 cops involved. Winnipeg Free Press; September 14, 1991. Pag 1

Ismon Marroquin

Crime stoppers pay off fund for cops. Winnipeg Free Press, September 14, 1991, Pag 4 By Paul Wiecek.

Whistle blower Shaver dreams of swapping B and E tools for badge. Winnipeg Free Press Pag 4. September 14, 1991.

Force escapes censure. Winnipeg Free Press September 14, 1991, Pag 4 By Kevin Rollason.

Big name lawyer gives tangled tale unusual twist. Winnipeg Free Press Sept 14, 1991, Pag 3; By Gordon Sinclair Jr.

Scandal puts cops into shock. Winnipeg Free Press, September 15, 1991, Pag 1. By Bruce Owen.

Hughes report delivers knockout blow. Winnipeg Free Press September 19, 1991, Pag 1 By Paul Wiecek.

Police handling of Pollock affair smacks of payback inquiry find. Winnipeg Free Press, September 19, 1991, Pag 1. By Donald Campbell.

Leave Quietly or be forced out Stephen told. Winnipeg Free Press; September 19, 1991, Pag 1 By Radha Krishnan Thampi.

Executioner Hughes didn't take off enough heads. Winnipeg Free Press, September 20, 1991; Pag 11 by Gordon Sinclair Jr.

Bitter complainant wants apology. Winnipeg Free Press, September 20, 1991, Pag 1; By Allison Bray.

Defiant Pollock Accepts no blame. Winnipeg Free Press September 20, 1991, Pag 1; By Donald Campbell and Bruce Owen.

Gunsmoke shrouds three dark years. Winnipeg Free Press Sept. 21, 1991, Pag 10; By Bruce Owen

Cash settlement hastened Stephen early departure. Winnipeg Free Press Sept. 21, 1991, Pag 1; By Radha Krishnan Thampi.

Suspended officer guilty of filching car speakers. Winnipeg free Press Sept. 26, 1991, Pag 13 By Terry Weber.

Black students accuse police of harassment. Winnipeg Free Press October 23, 1991, Pag 19; By George Nikides.

Shaken officer re-enacts shooting. Winnipeg Free Press, October 24, 1991, Pag A18; By Sue Montgomery.

Officers had nothing to hide lawyer. Winnipeg Free Press December 20, 1997, Pag A3. By Mike McIntyre.

Officer aided crimes chose sites, thief says. Winnipeg Free Press January 27, 1994, Pag B3; By Kevin Rollason.

City police shielding their own. Winnipeg Free Press April 15, 1995, Pag A2. By Paul Wiecek.

Mountie charged after pot found in desk. Winnipeg Free Press July 31, 1996, Pag A4, By Doug Nairne.

Cabbie dies after lengthy coma. Winnipeg Free Press, May 4, 1996, Pag A10. By Canadian Press.

Videotape captures violence at Boing. Winnipeg Free Press July 12, 1996, Pag 1. By Doug Nairne and Toni Davis.

We couldn't breathe, and we couldn't see. Winnipeg Free Press July 12, 1996, Pag 1. By Toni Davis.

Probe begins into police shooting. Winnipeg Free Press December 18, 1997. Pag 1. By Mike McIntyre and Leah Janzen.

Police at shooting refused booze tests. Winnipeg Free Press December 19, 1997, Pag 1: By Mike McIntyre.

Officer who killed dealer gave blood; other 7 had been at party. Winnipeg Free Press December 19, 1997, Pag 1. By Mike McIntyre.

Ismon Marroquin

Montreal officers fired over fatal assault. Winnipeg Free Press December 13, 1997, Pag A13. By Conway Daly.

How do you put a price on half a man's life? Winnipeg Free Press July 19, 1997. Pag A6. By Kim Guttermson.

Feisty senior backed. Man may be charged after intruder stabbed trying to brake into home. Winnipeg Free Press February 22, 1997. Pag A3

It's not about mistakes; it's about misconduct. Winnipeg Free Press July 19, 1997, Pag A4. By Gordon Sinclair Jr.

Milgaard cleared, Fisher on hooks. Winnipeg Free Press July 19, 1997, Pag 1. By David Kuxhaus and Melanie Verhaeghe. South African claims police beat him up. Winnipeg Free Press, February 21, 1998; Pag A3. By Gordon Sinclair Jr.

Police accused of ramming car, assault. Winnipeg Free Press, February 25, 1998, Pag 1. By Paul Wiecek.

LERA chief hit city police in road rage case. Winnipeg Free Press, February 26, 1998, Pag A4. By Paul Wiecek.

Police show support for suspended buddy, then pass us the bill. Winnipeg Free Press, September 26, 1998, By Gordon Sinclair Jr.

Acquitted man plans to sue police. Winnipeg Free Press, December 15, 1999, Pag A3. By John Lyons.

Epileptic dies after dose of pepper spray. Winnipeg Sun July 12, 2000, Pag 13. By Redaction.

Cops fatally shot man fingered in bar attack. Winnipeg Sun July 30, 2001, Pag 2. By Tracy McLanghlin.

Kenora police holding officer conduct report. Winnipeg Free Press December 2, 2004. By Mike McIntyre.

Pair of Kenora police officers face discipline in scandal. Winnipeg Free Press, December 9, 2004. By David Ruxhaus.

A promise made but not kept. Winnipeg Free Press, December 1, 2003, Pag B3. By Dan Lett.

Unsettled lies the crown. Winnipeg Free Press, December 1, 2003, Pag A10. By Editor Terence Moore.

Death called suicide by cop. Winnipeg Free Press, December 6, 2003, Pag A4. By Bruce Owen.

Are Canada's police forces getting dirtier? Winnipeg Free Press January 26, 2004. By James McCarten.

Why do city police still investigate themselves? Winnipeg Free Press December 6, 2005, Pag A4. By Gordon Sinclair Jr.

Prosecutors, police on hook on Driskell case. Winnipeg Free Press June 15, 2007, Pag A5. By Carol Sanders.

Ex-cop faces grow op charge. Winnipeg Free Press, June 28, 2007, Pag A5. By Mike McIntyre.

Plea deal messed up. Winnipeg Free Press, August 23, 2007. Pag A3 By Mike McIntyre.

Internet video of taser death sparks firestorm. Winnipeg Free Press, November 16, 2007. Pag A4. By Terri Theodore.

Justice ministers standing by stun guns. Winnipeg Free Press November 16, 2007, Pag A4. By Mary Agnes Welch.

Taser videos contradict RCMP: critic. Winnipeg Free Press November 16, 2007, Pag A3. By Camille Bains.

City won't stop use of tasers. Winnipeg Free Press November 16, 2007, Pag A3. By Aldo Santin.

Mounties can take action now. Winnipeg Free Press, August 13, 2009. Pag A10. By Redaction Gerald Flood.

Ismon Marroquin

Furor over photo radar just won't go away. Winnipeg Free Press, October 10, 2009. By Gordon Sinclair Jr.

Video contradicts police story about beating. News Canada Vancouver, July 9, 2010, Pag A5. By Camille Bains, Vancouver.

Former refugee claims harsh treatment at hands of police. Winnipeg Free Press, July 22, 2009; Pag B1. By Gordon Sinclair Jr.

14 years sentence angers police leadership. Winnipeg Free Press July 22, 2009, Pag B2. By Mike McIntyre and Gabrielle Giroday.

Man Tells of police beating. Winnipeg Free Press July 30, 2009, Pag A3. By Larry Kusch.

Senior's cellphone ticket stirs outrage. Winnipeg Free Press March 6, 2012. Pag A4. By Aldo Santin.

Police defend the issuing of ticket. Winnipeg Free Press March 7, 2012, Pag B1. By Bill Redekop and Aldo Santin.

The chief lied under the oath court told. Winnipeg Sun, May 1, 2012, News 3. By James Turner.

Still no closure in 2008 police shooting. Winnipeg Free Press, August 3, 2012, Pag A8.

Ontario cop guilty of brutal beating. The Canadian Press, June 22, 2013, Pag A8. By Canadian Press.

Police shooting of Toronto man a tragedy for all involved. Winnipeg Free Press, July 31, 2013. Pag A8. By Allison Jones.

Toronto Police didn't need to shoot teen.

Police mum on standoff death. Winnipeg Free Press, August 2, 2014. Pag A3. By Mike McIntyre.

De-escalating should be officers' top goal: expert. Winnipeg Free Press, August 2, 2014, Pag A3. By Kevin Rollason.

Brother removed rifle from Stella Avenue house years ago. Winnipeg Free Press, August 2, 2014, Pag A4. By Gordon Sinclair Jr.

Died of single gunshot, police finally reveal week after shooting. Winnipeg Free Press, August 7, 2014, Pag A4. By mike McIntyre.

Where is the transparency? Winnipeg Free Press, August 7, 2014, Pag A4. By Gordon Sinclair Jr.

Man killed by police depressed. Winnipeg Free Press, September 23, 2015. Pag B1. By Carol Sanders, Bruce Owen, Katie May and Mike McIntyre.

Killer behind Milgaard's conviction dies in prison. CTV News June 10, 2015.

Answers demanded from RCMP. Winnipeg Free Press, June 13, 2020. Pag A14. By Colette Derworiz and Lauren Krugel.

Egregious police tactics cause harm, activists say. Winnipeg Free Press, June 13, 2020. PagA14. By Daniela Germano.

"Kick likely saved his life". Winnipeg Free Press, June 13, 2020. Pag 1. By Ryan Thorpe.

Report into fatal police shooting withheld. Winnipeg Free Press, August 17, 2020. By Katia May.

Officer escaped charges despite IIU finding. Winnipeg Free Press, August 7, 2020, Pag A1 By Ryan Thorpe.

Watchdog absolves cop who shot machete-welding teen. Winnipeg Free Press, August 15, 2020. By Malak Abas.

Accused officer seeks to quash case over delays. Winnipeg Free Press, February 23, 2021. Pag B2. By Dean Pritchard.

Prosecutor alleges officer lied about seeing weapon during traffic stop. Winnipeg Free Press, March 25, 2021. Pag B2. By Dean Pritchard.

Ismon Marroquin

Winnipeg officer cleared in fatal shooting after domestic call. Winnipeg Free Press, May 6, 2021, Pag B3. By Ryan Thorpe.

Police face wrongful death suit alleging man wasn't threat. Winnipeg Free Press, June 26, 2021, Pag A11. By Dean Pritchard.

IIU clears city police in 2020 shooting. Winnipeg Free Press, June 13, 2022. Pag B3. By Erik Pindera.

RCMP taking in-custody death of Indigenous man seriously suggest in the past, it didn't. Winnipeg Free Press, January 24, 2022. Pag A5. By Niigaan Snclair.

Executive support amid inmate death draws fire. Winnipeg Free Press, January 25, 2022. Pag B3. By Carol Sanders.

The fundraiser for accused guard raised $50K before being pulled. Winnipeg Free Press, January 27, 2022. Pag A1. By Ryan Thorpe.

Man's arrest ugly side of policing: defense. Winnipeg Free Press, January 28, 2022. Pag B3. By Dean Pritchard.

Too late for wrongful conviction lawsuit, Judge. Winnipeg Free Press February 1, 2022; Pag A1. By Dean Pritchard.
    Dead toddler's mom wants police fired over domestic dispute response. Winnipeg Free Press, March 3, 2022. Pag A). By Mickey Djuric.

One Long Night
Andrea Pitzer

Innocence Canada

Printed in Canada